The Fantastic Fair

THE FANTASTIC FAIR

The Story of the California
Midwinter International Exposition
Golden Gate Park, San Francisco, 1894

By

Arthur Chandler
&
Marvin Nathan

POGO PRESS

ISBN 1-880654-03-2.

Library of Congress Catalogue Card No. 93-85326.

Illustration credits:
Midwinter Fair and The Golden State: Colored Art Views. California Education Series Nos. 1 and 2.
San Francisco: H. S. Crocker Co., 1894, for the colored plates on the front cover and
at pages 41 through 61.

The collection of I. W. Taber photographs, including the *I. W. Taber Album of Photographs of the
California Midwinter International Exposition,* from the San Francisco Room, San Francisco
Public Library, for the black and white photographs at pages facing page 1, 2, 3, 6, 11, 12,
13, 14, 20, 22, 24, 27, 28, 29, 30, 62, 65, 66 and 70.

Engravings made from photographs by A. W. Cornwall and A. W. Martin, from the *Scientific American
Magazine,* June 16, June 23, and July 14, 1894 at pages 16, 68, 9, and 18.

Lithograph on rear cover and at page 39 by Charles Graham, published by Winters Art
Lithographing Company of Chicago (1894), from the collection of Arthur Chandler.

Dedicated to the Memory of

RAYMOND H. CLARY

Scholar, Historian and Guardian Angel

of Golden Gate Park.

CONTENTS

ACKNOWLEDGMENTS

AUTHORS OF ANY BOOK such as this are always indebted to many other people who helped make their ideas a reality. Pat Akre, of the San Francisco Public Library, kindly made available numerous I. W. Taber photographs, including an exceptional Taber album of Midwinter Exposition views. Richard and Gladys Hansen, supervisors of the Raymond Clary Collection at the San Francisco History Museum, gave us invaluable help by allowing us access to that rich collection. Alfred Heller, editor and publisher of *World's Fair*, was kind enough to publish two essays on the exposition that served as the nucleus of the idea for this book. We also wish to thank Marilyn Blaisdell for providing us with copies of a number of the color lithographs used in *The Fantastic Fair*.

A number of years ago, the authors collaborated with Rodger Birt, Steve Dobbs, Art Hough and Richard Sammons on the production of a half-hour videotape on the Midwinter Exposition, called *The Fantastic Fair*. A good many of our ideas for the present book can be traced back to that wonderful collaboration.

Our wives, Jeanie Chandler and Gerry Nathan, read and re-read the manuscript, correcting errors and providing the kind of attention to detail and critique of the overall plan that have immeasurably improved the final manuscript.

Alvin Fine, the founder of San Francisco studies at San Francisco State University, has also been a guiding spirit behind this book. The support of the Alvin Fine Endowment at San Francisco State University has also been crucial for the publication of this book.

Timothy Drescher, our photographer and teaching colleague, gave us not only a rich set of visual images to work with, but some excellent advice on the best ways to display them in a text.

And finally, the authors pay their respect to the memory of Raymond Clary, who spent many years gathering material about the Midwinter Fair.

ARTHUR CHANDLER
MARVIN NATHAN
San Francisco,
July 1, 1993.

Director-General Michael H. de Young

In every respect, *San Francisco Chronicle* publisher Michael H. de Young was the father of the California Midwinter International Exposition. From his original inspiration in Chicago to hold the event, through all his subsequent efforts of fund-raising and supervision, de Young's personal energy and unrelenting efforts made the fair a reality.

The California Dreamer

IN MAY OF 1893, Michael H. de Young, the energetic publisher of the *San Francisco Chronicle*, stood at the entranceway to the California building at the World's Columbian Exposition in Chicago. He marveled at the sheer numbers of fairgoers who poured through the gates—crowds that enriched not only the exposition vendors, but the merchants of the city. The world's fair meant good business for Chicago.

Later, seated at his desk in the Mission Revival style California pavilion at the Chicago fair, de Young's thoughts turned to home. Matters were not well there. San Francisco, along with the rest of the nation, was suffering through a depression in 1893. Though the city boasted a growing population of over 300,000, its economy languished. Several banks had failed. Labor and management had clashed violently, and a legacy of division and bitterness brooded over the city's business enterprise. Local politics was dominated by "Blind Boss" Buckley and a swarm of imitators. And atop "Snob Hill," the grandiose mansions of the Big Four (Leland Stanford, Collis Huntington, Charles Crocker, and Mark Hopkins) lorded it over San Francisco, literally and symbolically resplendent reminders of the power of the railroad in American life. Warring factions in Chinatown fought bloody battles with each other, while suspicious outsiders denounced the quarter as a morass of opium dens and slave traders. The notorious Barbary Coast perpetuated the city's world-wide reputation as a haunt and a haven for cutthroats, thieves, and brigands who settled down in San Francisco for a long life of unimpeded crime.

But there was a brighter side to life in San Francisco. The spirit of West Coast freedom and panache was carried forth by a group of artists and fellow-travellers known as *Les Jeunes*. San Francisco's bohemians were writing and painting and regaling themselves with frolics and larks in the Barbary Coast and Chinatown between periods of poverty. The city was nurturing a genuine cultural renaissance.[1]

CALIF. MID-WINTER
EXPOSITION - 1894

**Knights of the Cleaver Float
on Butcher's Day**

Over 18,000 spectators turned out to see the city's meat cutters and their patriotically decorated float on parade. Attired in straw hats and aprons the "Knights of the Cleaver" and their wives accompanied their float on Butchers' Day at the fair, Wednesday, May 23, 1894. There were 28 major celebration days at the exposition and numerous smaller processions and special events. This celebration of Labor only a few months after a bitter union strike in San Francisco indicates one way in which the fair pulled the local community together. To the left rear of the Grand Court may be seen the Manufactures and Liberal Arts Building.

Local hotels, including the Palace and the Baldwin, were among the best-run in the country. San Francisco boasted a full season's worth of theater, opera, symphonic music and high-toned lecture series. In recent years, the city had played host to such highly-acclaimed writers as Oscar Wilde, Anthony Trollope, and Rudyard Kipling. San Francisco's schools flourished under the leadership of such educators as John Swett and Mary Kincaid. The Bay Area could boast of several institutions of higher learning, including the recently founded Stanford University. Clearly, the Boomtown and Barbary Coast images of the city were misleading as adequate portraits of San Francisco in the final decade of the nineteenth century. Despite a number of pressing economic and political problems, San Francisco possessed energy in abundant supply. There was a boldness of spirit in the city, and a population willing and eager to support and appreciate art and culture—to undertake the kind of enterprise so splendidly set forth at the Chicago world's fair.

As Commissioner of the California Exhibits and Vice President of the National Commission at the Columbian Exposition, de Young had ample op-

portunity to see the problems and the opportunities of his native city in perspective. Was there any way to heal the social and economic divisions that pitted so many factions against one other? How could some measure of unity be restored to the troubled community? The Columbian Exposition had clearly benefited Chicago in a number of ways. Perhaps San Francisco could profit from a similar experience.

De Young, wanting to capitalize on the impetus the Chicago fair had created, decided that San Francisco's exposition should open on January 1st, 1894, or in slightly over seven months.[2] San Franciscans would stage a great cooperative venture and make money for local entrepreneurs; the world would see the advantages of the city and the promise of the Golden State. The more de Young thought it over, the more excited he became.

But it had taken seven years to conceive, plan, and stage the Columbian Exposition. How could a newspaperman hope to bring about such a complex and expensive venture in seven months? A decade earlier, New Orleans businessmen had found to their sorrow that a world's fair was no guarantee of

President Harrison and de Young in front of Canadian Lodge

Former United States President Benjamin Harrison poses for a family portrait with Michael H. de Young in front of the Canadian Lodge at the fair. Harrison, in the top hat and with the gray beard, had left office in 1893 and was in the midst of a western tour during which he visited the exposition as well as other tourist sites in San Francisco. De Young, with the flower in his lapel, stands to the right of President Harrison.

WE MAY HAVE A FAIR.

Scheme of Californians at Chicago.

A Commercial Show in San Francisco.

Foreign Exhibitors Willing to Come After the Great Exposition.

Special Dispatch to the CHRONICLE.

CHICAGO, May 31.—If California is willing to make an effort she can have a World's Fair of her own in San Francisco at the close of the Chicago Exposition. Not a fair of such gigantic proportions as the Columbian show, but one which will be of far greater importance to California and the entire Pacific coast. It will be exactly what its name implies, the "Commercial World's Fair," and will consist of the cream of the Chicago Exposition.

All these statements may appear bold and will no doubt create an immense surprise, but none of them are improbable. It lies with the Californians themselves to make them possible. If California will, it is now within her power to carry out such an enterprise.

Portion of feature Article from the June 1, 1893 San Francisco Chronicle

success. Poor planning, bad weather, adverse political or economic conditions—there were many treacherous roads to failure, but no sure path to success.

However, Michael de Young was not to be denied his dream of "the Sunset City," as he would call the Midwinter Fair. He gathered together the San Francisco businessmen at the Columbian Exposition and set forth his dream. Though there were skeptics among them, the majority liked what they heard and immediately pledged over $40,000 for the enterprise, the largest single contribution of $10,000 given by financier and future San Francisco mayor James Duval Phelan. De Young sent telegrams to the governor of California (Henry Markham), the mayor of San Francisco (Levi Ellert), and numerous business organizations in order to solicit support for his grand scheme. A governing Board of Directors, headed by Director-General de Young, and an Executive Committee to supervise and plan the fair were appointed by a Citizens Committee of Fifty appointed by Mayor Ellert. The major motivation for the exposition would be economic. This motive was so explicit that the first working name for the exposition was "The Commercial World's Fair." On June 1, 1893, headlines in de Young's *San Francisco Chronicle* trumpeted the grand proposal.

The publicity department of the fair encouraged local printing companies to come up with ideas that would show San Francisco's winter climate in a favorable light. This they did—and with a good-natured slap at New York. One advertising card shows, on the left side of the picture, a solitary woman huddled up against the freezing snow outside a New York tenement. On the right side, an elegant young couple enjoys an open-air picnic with food and wine in front of the Conservatory of Flowers in Golden Gate Park. A second card shows a lovely young woman, whose hat announces her as "San Francisco," proffering a bouquet of fresh flowers to an aged, overweight man with frost for hair and icicles dripping from his beard. The old man is labeled "New York."[3]

Battles On The Home Front

THERE WERE THE inevitable skeptics, and one local critic labeled the proposed exposition "the Midwinter Fake." The first major challenge came from the friends and protectors of Golden Gate Park. The *Official History of the California Midwinter International Exposition* blithely glossed over the controversy:

> The fears of the Park Commissioners for the safety of their precious gems
> of forestry were allayed by the promises of the projectors that the desires
> of the Commissioners in this regard should be their special care. It was
> also pointed out that, just as the Columbian Exposition had transformed
> a disease-breeding marsh into a beautiful park, so should the Midwinter
> Exposition make the comparative wilderness of Concert Valley [an area in
> the southeast section of the Park] to blossom like the rose.[4]

In reality, though, the Exposition Executive Committee's decision was fiercely debated. Superintendent John McLaren was adamantly opposed to the plan, which he felt would lead to the desecration of his park's newly planted flora and set a precedent for holding large-scale commercial ventures in an area originally designed as a woodland retreat from urban life. McLaren's main ally was W. W. Stow, a millionaire friend of the park and a dedicated conservationist. At one critical meeting with the Golden Gate Park Commission, Stow denounced de Young's plan in ringing terms: "You come in here and destroy a tree that has been growing for twenty years. The fair will be here for six months. Trees will be here for a thousand years." De Young, though, was not to be stopped. He replied to Stow: "What is a tree? What are a thousand trees compared to the benefits of the exposition?"[5] Moving with energy and determination, he mobilized the resources of his newspaper, fanning local support into a flame. Hundreds of private contributors came forth, convinced that the Midwinter Fair could revitalize business and introduce San Francisco to the

Excavation Work on Fairgrounds Site
Despite the claims of wondrous new technologies at the Midwinter Fair, the job of clearing and leveling the grounds in Golden Gate Park's Concert Valley was done by the old fashioned efforts of horse-drawn sleds.

world as a city to be reckoned with. High society and working class alike pitched in to help finance the grand venture. The Golden Gate Opera Society gave the proceeds of their production of Gilbert and Sullivan's *The Pirates of Penzance* to the Exposition Executive Committee. The National Theater Company performed the new hit, *Evans and Sontag*, and presented the commission with another substantial contribution for the Midwinter Fair. A number of trade workers in the city met at the Potrero Opera House in September, 1893, and pledged one day's pay a week to help bring the fair into being. Even the newsboys of the city pooled their funds and contributed $2.74 to the venture.[6]

Moving with unprecedented speed, the Commissioners selected a sixty acre (later expanded to nearly triple that size) fairground in Golden Gate Park, had the site cleared, invited the exhibitors, made financial arrangements, held architectural competitions, selected winners, and supervised the building of over 180 structures—all within the span of a few months. And on January 27, 1894, a mere 26 days later than the date originally projected months before, the first American world's fair ever to be held west of Chicago opened its gates.

The Fantastic Fair

WHAT THE CROWDS saw at the California Midwinter International Exposition in 1894 was a Californian image of the world—the international drama in which San Francisco was determined to win its rightful place. De Young, afraid that the San Francisco fair would suffer by comparison if it tried to imitate the carefully coordinated Greco-Roman architecture of the Columbian Exposition, forbade any references to the Classical tradition in the major Midwinter Exposition buildings. San Francisco architects, though, were more than equal to the challenge. They were used to turning out exotic Victorian fantasies for their local nouveau riche clients, and therefore felt quite at home spinning out the multicultural extravaganzas that adorned the Grand Court of Honor at the Midwinter Fair.

The major buildings at the Chicago exposition all drew on the established architectural vocabulary of Europe and the ancient world. At San Francisco, highly personalized syntheses of world architecture flanked the Court of Honor. In Chicago, the main buildings were all white, in deference to their designer's notion of classical purity. In San Francisco, the "Sunset City" drew its color scheme from the spectrum that suffuses the skies over the Pacific horizon at evening time.

Thirty-six California counties, five American states, the Arizona Territory, and thirty-eight nations were represented by a building or an exhibit at the fair. The products displayed in the fair's buildings were judged in five major categories: agriculture and horticulture, manufactures, liberal arts, ethnology and invention, and the fine arts. Of the 2,083 prizes awarded, 1,325 went to American exhibitors and 758 to foreigners, with Spain accounting for 107 of the medals. The Committee on Awards, whose president was former San Francisco Mayor Frank McCoppin, appointed 213 jurors to judge the thousands of exhibits. The major buildings of the California Midwinter International Exposition were clustered around the Grand Court of Honor whose general outline

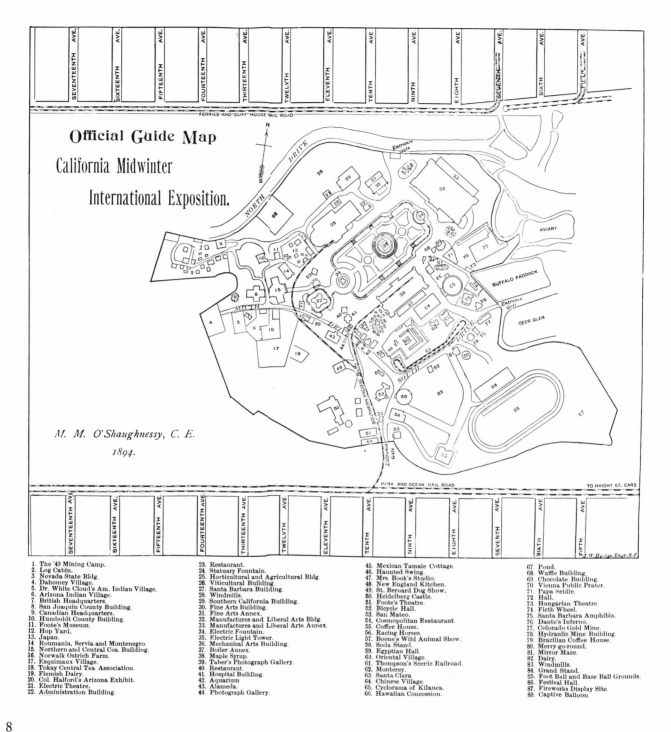

Official Guide Map

California Midwinter

International Exposition.

M. M. O'Shaughnessy, C. E.
1894.

1. The '49 Mining Camp.
2. Log Cabin.
3. Nevada State Bldg.
4. Dahomey Village.
5. Dr. White Cloud's Am. Indian Village.
6. Arizona Indian Village.
7. British Headquarters.
8. San Joaquin County Building.
9. Canadian Headquarters.
10. Humboldt County Building.
11. Foote's Museum.
12. Hop Yard.
13. Japan.
14. Roumania, Servia and Montenegro.
15. Northern and Central Cos. Building.
16. Norwalk Ostrich Farm.
17. Esquimaux Village.
18. Tokay Central Tea Association.
19. Flemish Dairy.
20. Col. Halford's Arizona Exhibit.
21. Electric Theatre.
22. Administration Building.

23. Restaurant.
24. Statuary Fountain.
25. Horticultural and Agricultural Bldg.
26. Viticultural Building.
27. Santa Barbara Building.
28. Windmills.
29. Southern California Building.
30. Fine Arts Building.
31. Fine Arts Annex.
32. Manufactures and Liberal Arts Bldg.
33. Manufactures and Liberal Arts Annex.
34. Electric Fountain.
35. Electric Light Tower.
36. Mechanical Arts Building.
37. Boiler Annex.
38. Maple Syrup.
39. Taber's Photograph Gallery.
40. Restaurant.
41. Hospital Building.
42. Aquarium
43. Alameda.
44. Photograph Gallery.

45. Mexican Tamale Cottage.
46. Haunted Swing.
47. Mrs. Book's Studio.
48. New England Kitchen.
49. St. Bernard Dog Show.
50. Heidelberg Castle.
51. Foote's Theatre.
52. Bicycle Hall.
53. San Mateo.
54. Cosmopolitan Restaurant.
55. Coffee House.
56. Racing Horses.
57. Boone's Wild Animal Show.
58. Soda Stand.
59. Egyptian Hall.
60. Oriental Village.
61. Thompson's Scenic Railroad.
62. Monterey.
63. Santa Clara
64. Chinese Village.
65. Cyclorama of Kilauea.
66. Hawaiian Concession.

67. Pond.
68. Waffle Building.
69. Chocolate Building.
70. Vienna Public Prater.
71. Papa Seidle.
72. Hall.
73. Hungarian Theatre.
74. Firth Wheel.
75. Santa Barbara Amphibia.
76. Dante's Inferno.
77. Colorado Gold Mine.
78. Hydraulic Mine Building.
79. Brazilian Coffee House.
80. Merry-go-round.
81. Mirror Maze.
82. Dairy.
83. Windmills.
84. Grand Stand.
85. Foot Ball and Base Ball Grounds.
86. Festival Hall.
87. Fireworks Display Site.
88. Captive Balloon.

still exists today as the Music Concourse in Golden Gate Park. Here, in the buildings and tower of this central court, San Francisco played out its dreams of imagination in the service of urban power and local boosterism.

At the southwestern end of the court stood Arthur Page Brown's Administration Building, a storybook fantasy that conjured up visions of fairy-tale palaces, much as Disneyland's castle does today. Its hexagonal tower, keyhole windows, and lacelike battlements inhabited an imaginative world far distant from the grandly sober and white buildings of the Chicago fair. Inside the building were the managers, clerks, and functionaries who looked after the daily business of the fair.

Facing this structure on the northeastern end of the Court of Honor was Brown's Manufactures and Liberal Arts Building—a cavernous structure which was the largest ever built in California up until that time (225 feet wide, 462 feet long). Modeled on the Palais de l'Industrie in Paris, the Manufactures and Liberal Arts Building recalled the glory of the first French Exposition Universelle, held in 1855. The building was made up of two distinct parts: an interior of glass-and-iron vaulting, which allowed large amounts of natural light to brighten the interior, and an outer sheathing of simulated stone, which gave an effect of solidity and massiveness.[7] The Arabic horseshoe arch over the entranceway echoed the similarly shaped portals on the Administration Building across the concourse—Brown's tribute to the coordinated planning of Daniel Burnham at the Chicago exposition for which the young California architect had designed the massive California Building. Here the fairgoers could see a full range of human ingenuity—from cut glass to corset stays, phonographs to flutes—arrayed before them.

On the southeast side of the Grand Court stood Edward Swain's Mechanical Arts Building. This colorful structure blended the architectures of the Near East, India, and the Slavic countries, with its minarets and onion domes soaring over ogival arches and intricate arabesques. Flags of the participating nations waved from the spires, and gave the building a festive international appearance. On display inside were the dynamos and large-scale engines that embodied the most current marvels of the Industrial Revolution. The best of Western technology housed in splendid palaces from faraway lands—that was San Francisco's dream of the ideal world of the future.

On the northwest side of the Concourse stood the last of the major buildings of the Midwinter Fair: Samuel Newsom's Horticultural and Agricultural Building, and C. C. McDougal's Fine Arts Building. Newsom's structure, with its iron and glass dome and Romanesque colonnade, was dubbed "generally speaking, the California Mission Style," and recalled the California Building at

The Ball of Gold

The mining section of the cavernous Mechanical Arts Building featured an enormous golden ball. This ball represented the total recorded gold mined in the state of California: 2,071 tons, worth $1,248,272,935.00 in the currency of the time. This volume represented one sixth of all gold mined worldwide from the sixteenth to the nineteenth century. The golden ball was a striking symbol of the natural wealth that created the basis of California's prosperity.

the Chicago fair. The glass dome was especially striking at night, when interior illumination made Newsom's creation glow like an immense jewel lit from within. The Horticultural and Agricultural Building housed an abundance of exotic plants, flowers, and even aquatic life. On one special day, snow was brought down from the Sierras and strewn throughout the corridors of the building to give the right backdrop for a special "sugaring-off" exhibition by the Vermont delegation.

The Fine Arts Building, located next to the Horticultural Building, was the most bizarre exhibition hall at the Midwinter Fair. Built in Egyptian Revival style by C. C. McDougal, the building was cursed with troubles from its inception. It was originally built to precisely rational specifications: 120 feet by 60 feet. But the clamor for exhibit space soon forced McDougal to add an annex, which added some 40 feet to the width. Nothing gives a clearer glimpse into the aesthetic sensibilities of turn of the century San Francisco than to read in the *Official History of the California Midwinter International Exposition* that "the [Fine Arts] building is simple in form and unpretentious in outline."[8] A pyramidal roof, projecting cornices surmounted by winged sphinxes, a recessed façade fronted by pseudo-Egyptian pillars, and all completely covered with imitation hieroglyphs—to any observer today, the Fine Arts Building would undoubtedly appear both pretentious and slightly ridiculous—a "theme building" in the manner of amusement park structures. After the Midwinter Fair closed in July of 1894, this historical fantasy was formally dedicated as the M. H. de Young Memorial Museum, San Francisco's first municipal art museum. Plagued by structural problems from the outset—museum officials constantly complained of leaks which could never be fixed—and overshadowed by Louis Christian Mulgardt's Spanish Revival "annex" to the museum built in 1918, McDougal's Egyptian palace was badly damaged in the 1906 earthquake and eventually fell to the wrecker's ball in 1928.[9]

In the very center of the Midwinter Exposition stood a tower which, at first view, seemed out of context with the other structures of the Grand Court of Honor. Furthermore, it was the only one of the major buildings not designed by a local architect. Frenchman Leopold Bonet's Electrical Tower was an obvious descendant of the Eiffel Tower,[10] with its soaring, unadorned steel girders and its lofty observation platforms. The electric tower was the brainchild of diplomat and designer Leopold Bonet, the French commissioner to both the Chicago and the San Francisco expositions. Bonet, head of a construction firm in Chicago, had tried to interest the Chicago commissioners in the idea of constructing a tower on the fairgrounds there, but his proposal was rejected. When he learned of the proposed Midwinter Fair, he wisely changed his tac-

The searchlight atop the Bonet Electric Tower was so powerful that one could sit at the foot of Prayer Book Cross Hill and read a newspaper by its light. The Tower itself was adorned with lights whose shifting patterns were controlled by a programmed metal cylinder.

tics. Following Gustave Eiffel's lead, Bonet formed a private syndicate of investors who provided him with an initial capital of $5,000 to build his tower in San Francisco. Investors in the syndicate were then to receive a percentage of the profits from the concession. In fact, Bonet's $5,000 was the very "first money paid into the treasury of the Exposition on account of a concession."[11]

Though the Bonet Tower was less than one third the size of the Eiffel Tower, it surpassed its Parisian counterpart in two respects. The Eiffel Tower was made of iron—a building material destined to give way to the greater structural advantages of steel. Bonet fashioned his tower of steel—making it the first structure of its kind in the United States. In addition, the Bonet Tower had more spectacular lighting effects. The Eiffel Tower had also been adorned with Thomas Edison's recent invention, the electrical light bulb, and even boasted a searchlight powerful enough to allow one to read a newspaper by its light at a distance of one mile from the Tower itself. But the Bonet Tower entranced fairgoers with its own special magic. During the day, the Electrical Tower stood as the central symbol for the promise of modern technology: power in the service of humankind. But at night the lights of the

Tower seemed to come alive. The girders were covered with interconnected strings of 3,200 incandescent light bulbs which were programmed to change by means of a coded metal cylinder. Diamonds, rosettes, crosses and circles flashed and winked out across the darkened girders. The *Official History* of the exposition reported that "One thousand of these were employed for outlining the tower, one thousand for the fixed decorative light effects, and twelve hundred in the changing geometrical designs."[12] And at the Tower's crown, "the most powerful searchlight in the world" shone across the young trees of the park, and illuminated the cross on Prayer Book Cross Hill. One commentator asserted that he could read a newspaper at midnight ten miles away by the light of the tower's beams—a substantial improvement over the Eiffel Tower's searchlight![13]

In the end, Bonet achieved his goals. The Tower made money as a concession and amply justified his faith in the ability of such an attraction to produce a profit. He had shown that Eiffel's crowning achievement could be, if not equaled, at least emulated, even in a remote and youthful American city such as San Francisco.

Bonet set one more precedent that would continue throughout San Francisco's history of hosting world's fairs. The Electrical Tower was what the French called a *clou*—a "spike" that gave an exposition a central, dominant

structure. Other great American world's fairs—New York in 1853-4, Philadelphia in 1876, Chicago in 1893—had their own striking and distinctive buildings. But none had had the spike that gave the world a memorable image of the dominant theme and meaning of the exposition. Eiffel's Tower was a self-conscious exclamation point to the Paris Exposition Universelle of 1889. Bonet's Tower served the same purpose for San Francisco in 1894, thereby creating a precedent for two later world's fairs—the Panama Pacific International Exposition with its Tower of Jewels, and the Golden Gate International Exposition's Tower of the Sun.[14]

There were other buildings at the exposition—some 180 in all, ranging from modest ticket-taking kiosks to the splendid reproduction of the Vienna Prater, with its theater, restaurant, concert hall, and booths for Austro-Hungarian wares. Some, like the Chinese Building designed by Martens and Cottey, made explicit reference to a single nation; others, like the Festival Hall, were pure architectural fantasy, with no clear precedents. Thanks to the careful planning by the Executive Committee, however, these other buildings did not detract from the basic impressiveness of the Court of Honor and its five central structures. Instead, all added to the variety of the exposition and gave visitors examples of architecture from cultures around the globe.

The Equilibrist

Juggling and balancing acts became very popular throughout the United States and Europe in the last half of the nineteenth century. French "equilibriste" Achille Philion astonished crowds with his ability to stand atop a huge ball as it descended a corkscrew ramp located next to the Bonet Electrical Tower on the Grand Court of Honor.

Instructive Amusements

EVER SINCE THE French Exposition Universelle of 1867, world's fairs had offered visitors a chance to combine education with amusement. Critics of a more sober turn of mind criticized this trend, asserting that the addition of such frolics gave an exposition the vulgar air of a peddler's bazaar or a gypsy carnival. But exposition organizers realized that it was the "Midway," or amusement section, that often spelled the difference between financial success or failure for an entire exposition.

Borrowing heavily from the Parisian and Chicago fairs, the Midwinter Exposition offered a large and diverse amusement zone called the Midway Plaisance. One of the most ingenious of the amusements at the Midwinter Fair was "the Haunted Swing." Twelve to fifteen visitors at a time would pay their admissions, then proceed to their seats on a large swing situated in the middle of a comfortably furnished parlor. The swing was suspended from a bar which crossed the room below the ceiling. Once settled in their places, visitors looked around at their surroundings and saw familiar objects: chairs, dressers, pictures on the wall, and a lighted kerosene lamp upon a table. Then, little by little, the swing appeared to move back and forth. It described greater and greater arcs until at last the astonished participants appeared to be hanging upside down in the room—yet their hats remained on their heads! Around and around they seemed to go—many passengers became dizzy, and some even fainted at this point. Finally the swinging ceased, and the giddy visitors reeled from the room. In fact, the swing had remained stationary. The walls and ceiling of the room itself were mounted on a revolving drum with all the furnishings and fixtures cleverly and securely bolted down. The room revolved around the stationary swing; but so complete was the conviction that a room could not revolve, and that a kerosene lamp would spill its contents (it contained no oil: a hidden incandescent light bulb provided the light), no one suspected that the room itself rotated. Even those who came away half ill from

The Haunted Swing

This popular attraction featured a furnished room in which visitors, seated in a large swing, seemed to revolve and hang upside down. Though in fact the swing remained stationary and the room rotated on a metal drum, the illusion was so convincing that many visitors emerged from the attraction complaining of being dizzy and faint.

the experience had to admit that the "Haunted Swing" was one of the most convincing illusions they had ever encountered.

Many of the exhibits in the Midwinter Fair Midway would be familiar to anyone who has visited an amusement park today. But in a world's fair held a century ago, even the amusements had to be justified with some sense of moral purpose. "Dante's Inferno," one of the central attractions of the Midway, was a house of horrors in the traditional American carnival mode. But to the writers of the *San Francisco Wasp,* the visitor who passed through the gaping jaws of the dragon at the entranceway would encounter the poetic vision of the great Italian poet Dante Alighieri:

> No painted imitation decorates the walls, but figures life-size and bearing all the semblance of an immortal part convey to the spectator's mind some idea of what Dante had in mind when describing the torments and

horrors of hell. It is a scene at once of terror and sublimity, lost souls writhing in agony, and malicious demons adding to their misery by indescribable aggravations of their torture. To the spectator there comes a fear of the unknown in viewing the scenes enacted here.[15]

We have only to compare the experience of going through a carnival spookhouse today with the description quoted above to get a sense of contrast between the late nineteenth and the late twentieth century. Underlying the experience of "Dante's Inferno" at the Midwinter Fair was the almost universal belief in the existence of an afterlife, and the prospect of everlasting damnation as the reward for a misspent life. A century later, a comparable funhouse scene is merely a humorous trip through a sleazy world of poor illusions that only barely tug at the primordial fear that such scenes once inspired.

There were other illusions in the Midway that inspired awe of a different kind. The most famous of these tricks was "Roltair's New Illusion of Pharaoh's Daughter," an attraction that astonished everyone who had the good fortune to witness it. Spectators would see an apparently lifeless marble statue become a lovely young lady before their very eyes. The great French magician Robert Houdin originated this illusion, but performed it only in the dimness of gaslit interiors. Roltair's improved version enhanced the vividness of the illusion, and observers often gasped with astonishment as the transformation took place. "The change is incomprehensible," remarked the reporter for the *Wasp*, "and sets all one's ideas of the eternal fitness of things at naught."[16] Roltair's illusion was housed in the Egyptian Hall, one of many such bizarre architectural fantasies at the Midwinter Fair. Close by on the Midway was yet another Egyptian evocation: Cairo Street. The original Cairo Street was a feature both at the Parisian Exposition Universelle of 1889 and the Columbian Exposition of 1893. For the French, the street provided visitors an opportunity to experience a kinesthetic sense of the Mideast, where they had long been establishing an empire. But for San Franciscans, Cairo Street conjured up visions of the mysterious Near East. Native Egyptians led camels up and down, offered passers-by lemonade from huge tanks strapped to their backs, and beckoned them to enter into a theater to witness Little Egypt's scandalous belly dance. The goal was to surround the visitors with the total ambiance of an Egyptian marketplace. Cairo Street is an important ancestor of the theme park in California.

"Roltair's Illusion of Pharaoh's Daughter," the Egyptian Hall, Cairo Street, the belly dance, the Fine Arts Building—the Midwinter Fair teemed with references to Egypt. What was the attraction of this ancient land for the inhabitants of a Pacific Coast metropolis? Part of the fascination was no more than the

The Firth Wheel and Dante's Inferno

The Firth Wheel was the Midwinter Fair's answer to—and imitation of—the Ferris Wheel from the Columbian Exposition in Chicago. Local wags scoffed at the borrowing, asserting that "It's not the Firth Wheel: it's the second wheel!" Less than half the size of its predecessor, the Firth Wheel was 100 feet in diameter, carried 160 people and was driven by a 200 horse power steam engine. Though smaller than the Ferris Wheel, the builders cleverly placed it on a rise so that the Firth actually took riders to an altitude of 385 feet, 127 feet higher than the Chicago version. "Dante's Inferno" with its monster-faced entrance, featured "bottomless pits and dancing skeletons." Some visitors found a stern moral warning in its depiction of the torments of hell.

18

familiar Western attitude, compounded of attraction and repulsion, for the strange customs of the non-Christian nations of the world. San Franciscans watching the belly dance could indulge in both voyeurism and a sense of cultural superiority at the same time. Seeing the camels plod up and down the street, led by natives clad in Egyptian dress, visitors stared openly at the spectacle and enjoyed the sheer strangeness of it, while at the same time they could contrast such exotica with the American and European industrial exhibits in the Liberal and Mechanical Arts buildings.

But Egyptian culture held other resonances for Europeans and Americans. For them, Egypt at the turn of the nineteenth century was typified by camels, belly dancers and picturesque costumes. In addition, informed San Franciscans knew contemporary Egypt as a harassed country besieged by British, Italian, Turkish, Abyssinian, and French forces, all contending for power. But ancient Egypt carried a universe of mysterious associations. The ancient hieroglyphs, though partially opened to understanding by the finding of the Rosetta Stone, were still incompletely interpreted, and offered translators nothing like the certainty of Greek or Latin texts. As a result, the ancient glory of Egypt was surrounded by tantalizing mystery, redolent of magical and mysterious rites, fabulous treasures, and forgotten lore.

There was a decidedly political agenda at the Midwinter Fair Midway. Ancient Egypt might be a source of mystical wisdom. But modern Egypt was a colony, a once powerful nation now subjected to the colonial ambitions of European nations. The African country of Dahomey (now called Benin) was also represented at the fair—but presented as the home of savages recently conquered by France. The photographs of the Dahomeans taken at the exposition show the men waving their weapons, while the women sit calmly before the camera with their breasts bare. Black San Franciscans, on the other hand, treated the Dahomeans as envoys from a foreign country, and invited them to local lodges for formal receptions.

Eskimos and Hawaiians were also present—as native inhabitants of America's own burgeoning colonial empire. The Alaskan village featured Eskimos, sled dogs, and imitation igloos fashioned from plaster staff. In 1894 the Alaskan exhibit attracted only moderate attention; had visitors known of the Gold Rush that would invade the Klondike only three years later, more attention might have been paid to the exhibits from Alaska, America's northernmost territory.

The Hawaiian village was far more attractive—in part, no doubt, because of the "Hawaiian dancing girls clad in their peculiar costumes."[17] Once lured in by the undulating grass skirts, however, the visitor encountered a well-

Dahomey Tribesmen

French explorer and entrepreneur Xavier Pené brought "his Dahomeyan Amazons" attraction directly from their successful tenure at the Columbian Exposition. For the Buffalo world's fair of 1901 Pené organized still another "African Village."

designed display showing the history of the native Kamehameha dynasty, bamboo dwellings, war weapons and coffee trees. But the real attraction was the "cyclorama" of the crater of Kilauea, with its realistic simulation of burning lava lakes and surges of steam. At the edge of the simulated crater was a cadre of priests intoning prayers to the god of the volcano, and a choir of native musicians and singers invoking the deity. However, this exhibit too had its political sequel. The first scholarly discussion, as reported in the *California Midwinter Exposition Illustrated* newspaper, was held as part of the Midwinter Fair's cultural program and took place on January 25, 1894, two days before the exposition opened. Its topic was whether or not the United States should annex the Hawaiian Islands!

The Immoral Exposition?

IN SPITE OF THE efforts of the Midwinter Commissioners to keep all the amusements "family-oriented," a number of people cried out against what they perceived to be the indecency of many of the features of the exposition. The gum-girls, for example, who could be seen skittering around the fairgrounds smiling and hawking samples of chewing gum, raised the wrath of one visitor:

> I went to the Midwinter Fair this week. The grounds looked very pretty, but I was disgusted with those pert gum, candy, and flower girls in short dresses. Most of them are really women and should not be allowed to go about exposing their limbs in such a bare-faced manner, and the ridiculous fools of men all seem to like it. The way I saw some of them going on with the men was shocking and I think I shall have to write Director-General M. H. de Young about the matter. I'm sure if he knew, he'd stop them right away.[18]

There is the distinct possibility that the above piece is satirical, directed against other such people who made this kind of objection. But there were also visitors who objected to the gum girls on other grounds:

> The request has been made that visitors to the grounds will refrain from whistling "Two Little Girls in Blue." For a time the wonder was why this air should be so popular, but the mystery was soon solved. The concessionaire who has the sale of chewing gum dressed up a number of young ladies in short navy blue dresses trimmed with gold braid, navy caps, black stockings and tan shoes. The combination is a pretty one, and as the girls travel in couples an everlasting whistle of the popular air ("Two Little Girls in Blue") is the outcome.

The Gum Girls

Popular opinion was divided on the ubiquitous gum girls who hawked their chewable wares throughout the fairgrounds. Some found them charming, with their coordinated costumes and cheery dispositions. Others found their costumes too risqué, or their constantly-repeated songs an annoyance.

At first it was amusing and the fair gumsellers joined in the merriment. Finally it became monotonous, as nearly every time a purchase was solicited an idiotic stare and a more or less outrageous rendition of the air would be the answer.[19]

However, it was not the gum-girls, but the scandalous "belly dances" that brought forth the most vehement expression of outraged public morality. Yet, as we see in the following piece, there may be more than a hint of fascination couched in terms of moral censure. Here is the report on the visit by the Society for the Suppression of Vice to the Turkish dances at the Midwinter Exposition:

The Society for the Suppression of Vice, upon the arrival here of those pretty but naughty Turkish dancing girls, determined that they would not permit them to demoralize the morality of the average San Franciscan by

22

giving public exhibitions. At a recent meeting of the society it was moved that in the interest of fair play a committee of three should attend the dances in question and decide whether they were really immoral or not. But as each member of the society expressed a desire to be a member of the committee, it was decided in the interest of harmony to attend as a committee of the whole.

The girls gave them the exhibition in their rooms, and in justice to the society, it is but proper to state that every member did his duty by being present. At the conclusion of the performance it was the unanimous opinion of the gentlemen that it was hardly possible to agree upon a verdict as to the moral status of the dances without witnessing another trial, and in accordance with this sentiment a second performance was equally well attended.[20]

In the end, the Society suspected that the dancers were withholding the really lascivious parts of their dances for fear that the committee members would not allow them to perform. Ever zealous, the Society for the Suppression of Vice decided not only to keep monitoring the dances throughout the exposition, but to keep the Hawaiian hula dancers under close observation as well.

The Exposition Illustrated Newspaper and the Prune Knight

There were three official exposition newspapers distributed regularly on the fairgrounds. The one illustrated here, rather pretentiously titled the *California Midwinter Exposition Illustrated Series of the Pacific States: The Authentic Pictorial Journal of the Exposition,* was issued bimonthly in March and April and monthly from May to July of 1894. It contained lengthy stories keeping fairgoers informed about important exhibits and recent events, as well as numerous illustrations, many of them taken from I. W. Taber photographs. Depicted is the "Prune Knight," one of the more bizarre and popular exhibits at the fair. This life-sized fruit sculpture, located in the Santa Clara County Building, was one of several such pieces of "food art" at world's fairs which were used to promote foodstuffs from various regions of the country in dramatic terms. This medieval warrior, who had put in an appearance in the California Building at the Columbian Exhibition the year before, was actually a combination of prunes, apricots, pears, nectarines and plums, all fruits grown in abundance by Santa Clara County farmers.

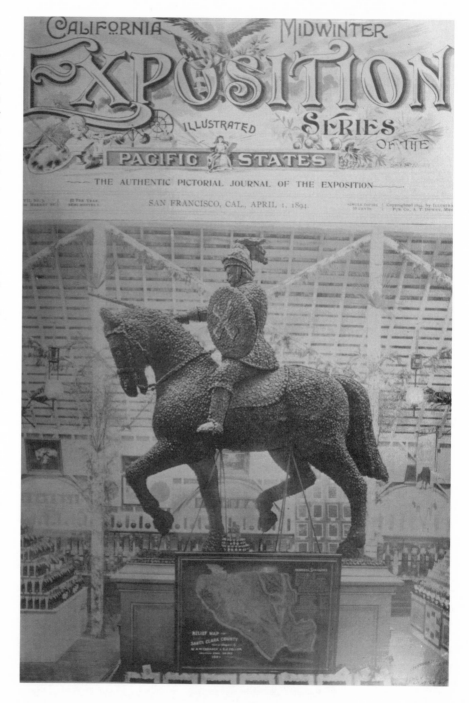

California Abundance

THERE WAS AT LEAST one major advantage in holding a world's fair in San Francisco so close on the heels of the Chicago Exposition: many national and foreign exhibitors were persuaded to ship their treasures to the West Coast for another six months of exhibition before returning home. Because the Midwinter Fair organizers could make arrangements with prospective exhibitors in Chicago without having to travel or correspond with foreign governments around the globe, the task of lining up participants was vastly easier. Exhibits, commissioners, concessions—all could be sent to California with a minimum of fuss. The net result was that the Commissioners of the Midwinter Fair could lay before the public a sizable representation of world culture. Art and artifacts, industrial exhibits and exotic amusement concessions—a treasure that had taken Chicago some years to assemble—all were there in Golden Gate Park for San Franciscans to contemplate and admire from January to July of 1894.

Another real advantage—one that the Midwinter Fair managers played up for all it was worth—was the mild climate of the city during the winter months. Ironically, though, a severe snowstorm in the Sierra mountains delayed the arrival of the exhibits from Chicago, so the opening date of the Midwinter Exposition had to be postponed almost four weeks. But once the exhibits arrived, the climate of San Francisco more than compensated for the Sierra blizzards. The mild temperature and verdant winter landscape mightily impressed visitors from the Midwest and East Coast. To see a section of the country that turned green in winter must have been a revelation to visitors from Minnesota or Vermont, Paris or Moscow. Indeed, the heavy migration to San Francisco during the last several years of the nineteenth century might be attributable to the reputation that California had acquired as a veritable Eden in all seasons. Between 1890 and 1900, San Francisco's population jumped from 300,000 to well over 400,000 inhabitants. The theme of Benign Abun-

The Rescue of Pawnee Jack

"Pawnee Jack to the Rescue" was an old western scene shown daily at the "Mining Camp of Forty-Nine" attraction. In the tradition of nineteenth century *tableaux vivants,* this highly posed playlet depicted the mountain man rescuing a wounded sheriff, a second compatriot and a maiden in distress from eight rather lethargic Native Americans. Such productions underscored both California's frontier past and contemporary racial attitudes.

dance featured so prominently at the fair must certainly have had some part in drawing those newcomers to the city.

In local exhibits, Californians capitalized on the natural advantages of their state, and the colorful history that Bret Harte had popularized in his gold rush stories. One exhibit showed the excitement of the gold rush days, and even gave visitors a chance to be held up at gunpoint (all in fun, of course) during a stagecoach ride. Or mostly fun: on one occasion, the stagecoach overturned, injuring several passengers, thereby giving them a real taste of the actual perils of stagecoach travel in California.

Another exhibit showed off local vintages, and dared European wine makers to match the quality of California wines. "Only second to her mines/ Are California's vines," ran the adage of California growers. Inside the Viticulture Building the visitor could contemplate a contemporary engraving that showed an aged man representing Europe, his head wreathed with a circlet of grape

leaves, accompanied by a cavorting faun. His head is bowed, and in his right arm he holds a thyrsus, the symbolic staff carried by Bacchus, god of wine. He is surrendering the thyrsus to a young man accompanied by a lady clothed in an American flag. The lady is America, the young man is California. It is the destiny of the young state, the artist implies, to inherit the great tradition of wine-growing from a tired and aging Europe. There is no record of what European visitors to the Viticulture Building thought of this brazen presumption. But the intention on the part of the Exposition Commissioners is clear. The engraving and the Viticulture Building itself were unmistakable announcements that California fully intended to become a major wine-producing state. And, in the course of the succeeding years, so it did, increasing from the 17 million gallons of the 1890s to 400 million gallons today.

Exposition buildings housed some truly whimsical manifestations of local pride. There was a gigantic elephant, a gift of Los Angeles, fashioned from half

The Mining Camp of Forty-Nine

"The Mining Camp of Forty-Nine" recreated several Gold Rush memories on the main street of a settlement supposedly located at the foot of Mount Shasta. Along with a stagecoach station, livery stable, hotel, restaurant, saloon and log cabins, there was a dance hall, depicted here, where miners could perform with the "ladies" present such dances as the reel, the quadrille, waltzes, polkas and gallops.

Viticulture Building Interior

The Viticulture Building, whose entrance was a gigantic oak barrel, had an interior designed like a traditional German Weinstube with vine-covered rafters, large written inscriptions on the wooden walls of the tasting room, and plaster casts of Bacchus and Mercury. Its shelves featured the finest wines from throughout the world, including such California vineyards as Inglenook, Cresta Blanca and Haraszthy. Indeed, over three dozen local wineries had displays. Several of these vintages won awards, making a powerful statement about California's challenge to European vintners.

a ton's worth of walnuts. Its saddle cloth, howdah, and trappings were outlined with citrus fruits, peanuts, and corn. There was an obelisk of oranges, and even a towering medieval knight fashioned mostly out of prunes![21] Behind the whimsy, however, there was a serious message. These fantastic exhibits told the visitors that California could produce anything, even during winter months, in unlimited abundance.

It is tempting to guess why the food growers' concession chose such exotic forms for their fruits and nuts. Why not a California Grizzly or a Statue of Liberty? Whatever the reason, they were in keeping with the exotic themes of the fair. An obelisk of oranges might remind the visitor of the Egyptian Hall or the Fine Arts Building; the walnut elephant might call up visions of India expressed architecturally in the Mechanical Arts Building; the prune knight perhaps recalled the turrets and crenelations of the Administration Building or the Manufactures and Liberal Arts Building. Or the forms might suggest the

Part of the Los Angeles Country exhibit was a life-size model of an elephant covered in walnuts. The whimsy of the display should not hide the message inherent in all such exhibits at the exposition: California could produce any goods, familiar or exotic, in almost unlimited abundance.

place of origin of the product: oranges from the Near East, walnuts from Afghanistan and the northwest Himalayas, etc. But one can only speculate. The organic sculptures may well have been the products of simple whim on the part of the creators. The tradition of displaying agricultural abundance in sculptural form, borrowed from earlier American expositions, would be continued after 1894 by other states in exhibitions and fairs. Forts made of apples or canoes of butter were common. South Dakota's Corn Palace, redecorated with new ears of corn each summer, continues that tradition.

South Sea Islanders

This proud group of Samoan men and women or, as they were referred to at the fair, South Sea Islanders, pose in tribal dress with drums and oars. As it was at the Chicago exposition, the Samoan village was located in the amusement Midway where visitors could witness the tribal dances, native crafts and colorful processions of these "pre-civilized" people. Though the Samoans seldom left the fairgrounds, one wonders what they must have thought of the "civilization" which staged the exposition.

Patrons Of Ideas

THE PLANNERS OF the Midwinter Exposition believed that San Francisco's first world's fair should do more than house exhibits and provide amusement. A serious exposition, they felt, should also sponsor serious discussions of ideas by bringing together respected authorities in the fields of economics, politics, religion, literature, education and science. Such events, following the precedent of previous world's fairs, were called "congresses." Millionaire patron of the arts and future San Francisco mayor James Phelan was chosen president of the Midwinter Exposition Congresses Committee, whose task was to organize and promote discussions that would "advance the cause of Progress in human endeavor."

Like the buildings and exhibits of the exposition, the congresses—some of which were held on the fairground, some in downtown San Francisco—were eclectic and world-wide in scope. Also like the buildings, many of the congresses devoted sessions to the specifically Californian setting of their subject. Just as each of the major buildings at the fair blended architectural motifs from various cultures, so the congresses sought a regionally-based, European-inspired, global perspective in the range of topics they considered. Economists discussed "The Market for California Breadstuffs," as well as "Monetary Affairs in the United States" and "England's Relation to Monetary Affairs in India." The Literary Congress opened with a passionate defense of California regional literature; then came sessions devoted to the entirety of English and American literature; at the conclusion, auditors heard a scholarly paper on "Prehistoric Malayan Literature."

But the liveliest of the exposition meetings was the Woman's Congress. The fair organizers had already encountered some strong sentiments from women about their lack of presence on the planning committees. "The Midwinter Fair people have run afoul of the woman question thus early," commented a writer for one of the Sacramento newspapers. "Certain sex-conscious women are howling because no provision has been made for a board of 'lady managers,' and for a distinctive women's department."[22] Since the Chicago exposition had an entire Woman's Building, designed by a woman architect and devoted entirely to feminine exhibits, it is likely that local feminists felt that the Midwinter Fair should do no less in support of women's issues.

But the protests produced no Board of Women Managers and no Woman's Building. Local supporters of such causes had to be content with a congress. Discussions were centered around those activities which, in the world of the 1890s, constituted acceptable activities for women: education, charities and missionary work, and the decorative and pictorial arts. However, as the discussions progressed, topics ranging from educational reform to the immigration question to the disadvantages of female costume in the workplace to women's suffrage were hotly debated. A budding militancy pervaded many of the meetings, especially in the panel devoted to the topic of exclusion of women from the business world. But the very liveliness of such debates led the fair Directors and the local newspapers to count the Midwinter Fair Congresses a resounding success. Certainly the Woman's Congress was the first major forum in which San Francisco women were able to begin to engage their male counterparts as equals in sustained and serious discourse on significant social issues.

The African-American Presence

THE MIDWINTER FAIR featured a special "Afro-American Day" with festivities designed to recognize the many voices of the black community in San Francisco, which then numbered just under 2,000 people. The day began with a military parade, and led one commentator to reflect that "it was the first time a colored military company with muskets and uniforms had been seen in California."[23] Following the outdoor activities, participants and spectators moved to the Festival Hall. A list of the day's events reveals a glimpse of the variety and range of such affairs a century ago:

> Overture, by Midwinter Exposition Band; introductory remarks, Reverend W. B. Anderson of Stockton; remarks, by S. Wilson; address by Director-General de Young; music by the Exposition Band; address, by T. B. Morton, President of the Afro-American League; address, by Reverend Obediah Summers; tenor solo, by Oscar T. Jackson; paper on "The Higher Education of Women," by Miss A. Hall; piano solo, by Mrs. Pauline Burns of Oakland; oration, by Reverend Tighman Brown; music by the Exposition Band; address, by Dudley Seebree; recitation, by Miss Alma Norrell; piano solo, by Professor John Williamson; dramatic recitation, by James Summers; vocal solo, by Miss Rosa Sugg; piano solo, by Miss Hattie Overton; trombone and cornet selections, by Ed. E. Jones; music by Exposition Band; benediction by Reverend S. H. Smith. . . .
>
> The Afro-American Day exercises will close with a ball tonight in Festival Hall. There will be a select programme of dances, including the Spanish York, La Marjoberline, the Oxford Minuet, the Illinois and the Berlin.[24]

For the modern reader there are some striking features about this list: the mixture of music and spoken words in a formal gathering; the variety of topics covered; and the sheer length of the program. It is especially interesting to note that the main paper delivered dealt with the education of women—not the education of African-Americans, or even the education of African-American women. It was apparently the case that the music and the range of topics addressed reflected not only the specific internal concerns of the black community but also the universal range of their interests as participants in the American community.

Nevertheless, much of the actual content of the main addresses was concerned with race relations. In his keynote address, de Young praised the efforts at self-improvement and self-advancement on the part of African-Americans, and noted what he conceived to be an improvement in their lot since the Civil War. De Young's optimistic view was qualified in a subsequent speech by Reverend Obediah Summers from Oakland, who commented that "if the mechanics' unions and other industrial organizations were open to us we might have had a building which would have been a credit to us and to the Fair"[25]—a clear reference and objection to the color barriers in the skilled trades. Nevertheless, Reverend Summers found that prejudice against his people was gradually disappearing in America. He concluded, addressing his remarks directly to de Young:

> America is holding out its hand to us as you did today. There was a time
> in this history of this nation when I could not stand on the same platform
> with men of another race or reply to your address. We did not bring thou-
> sands here today, but we came ourselves to show our appreciation of your
> work, and may God bless you, Sir.[26]

African-American pride found several outlets at the Midwinter Exposition. Perhaps the most striking instance was the effort on the part of one woman, Mrs. Case, to have an exhibit of work by black students given space in the Manufactures and Liberal Arts Building. She appealed successfully to the Executive Committee of the fair and placed an exhibit by a black Christian student organization from Georgia's Atlanta University in a section adjacent to an exhibit from Yale University in the second floor gallery. The Atlanta exhibit consisted of wood joining, printing, and scrap sewing done by students from all grades at the school. The exhibit attracted much praise and was awarded a first prize medal by the judges.

Intellectual Exchange

THE LOVER OF WISDOM or lively debate could choose from a large variety of offerings at the Midwinter Fair. Some, like the meetings of the American Medical Association and the California Teachers' Association, were the regular annual meetings of these associations held in conjunction with the exposition. Others, like the Dental Congress, were scheduled especially for the Midwinter Fair. Still others, while not receiving exposition sanction, capitalized on the crowds of visitors to patronize their meetings. One of these unsanctioned events was the Temperance Congress, held in a tent erected at Seventh and Mission Streets in the city. The mood of these gatherings was often fervently missionary, featuring impassioned rhetoric and tearful confessions from reformed drinkers. But the revivalist tenor of the Temperance Congress was at least partially balanced by the appearance of some distinguished speakers, including David Starr Jordan, president of Stanford University.

Other groups that might not have gained a foothold in the exposition by themselves managed to get a hearing under the auspices of the Religious Congress. Most of the meetings held in the Religious Congress were not controversial and confined themselves to topics such as "The Fatherhood of God and the Brotherhood of Man," "Historic Theism," and "The Reciprocity of Religion and Art." Some speakers, though, pushed their own agendas. "Christ Not Krishna" devoted itself to an exposition of the superiority of Christianity over "Hindooism." Another lecturer spoke on "The Church and Municipal Reform" and raised the possibility of creating a national church in the United States.

The profusion of congresses bespoke a parallel interest in the arts and education of a city in the midst of its own literary and artistic renaissance. *Les Jeunes*, the San Francisco version of the nineteenth century bohemian movement, was coming to full bloom during the middle years of the 1890s and was publishing an energetic little journal, *The Lark*, which would achieve national circulation and critical praise. Frank Norris was hard at work on *McTeague*—perhaps the definitive novel of San Francisco during those years, and one of the great social novels of nineteenth century America. Sculptures began to line Market Street—an anticipation of the City Beautiful movement that came to the city soon after the turn of the century. Opera, symphonic music, the theater, and fine publishing houses thrived in a San Francisco eager to take its place as a cultural leader among American cities.

Color Illustrations

Bird's Eye View of the Fantastic Fair

THIS MAJESTIC OVERVIEW of the Midwinter Fair is taken from a chromolithograph by Charles Graham. We can clearly see the overall plan of the exposition, with the major buildings forming a stately quadrangle and the Bonet Electrical Tower providing the spike at the center. In the distance, San Francisco Bay and the Marin Headlands provide a stunning backdrop for the "Sunset City" in Golden Gate Park.

Horticultural and Agricultural Building

THE HORTICULTURAL AND AGRICULTURAL BUILDING which stood on the northwestern side of the Grand Court of Honor between the Japanese Tea Garden and the Fine Arts Building housed the thousands of floral, farming and aquatic exhibits present at the fair. Its architect was Samuel Newsom, one of California's leading builders of Victorian houses since the 1870's. He designed an exhibition hall 400 feet long and 200 feet wide for an economical $58,000. Since most of the exhibits in his building were living things needing sunlight, Newsom placed a gigantic glass dome measuring 99 feet high and 100 feet wide over the center of the structure. Like the other major buildings at the fair, this one too was eclectic in its visual character. The triple arched entrance, the round window above, and the massive walls suggested a heavy reliance on Romanesque cathedrals. The long, low roofs covered with red clay tile were reminiscent of California Mission style. The open arcade surrounding the building where constantly changing floral, plant and aquatic exhibits were shown harkened back to the traditional monastic architecture of Spain. Only the two blue-tinted glass domes flanking the main entrance and the great ferro-vitreous dome in the center broke the southern European mood of the Horticultural and Agricultural Building. The central portion of the structure's interior lay under this massive dome with the remainder of the interior taken up by a spacious, encircling gallery. At the rear of the building was a large hall used for special county and district exhibits and for meeting rooms of the various awards committees. Despite local pretensions to national leadership in industry and the arts, agriculture was still California's most important business and export in 1894. And so, it is accurate to say that the Horticultural and Agricultural Building housed the most significant commodities the Golden State exhibited at the Midwinter Fair. Most of the site where this impressive edifice once stood is today occupied by the new de Young Museum.

Japanese Village (Tea Garden)

THE JAPANESE VILLAGE, popularly known as the Japanese Tea Garden, though much altered over the past 100 years, is the only significant architectural vestige of the Midwinter Exposition remaining in Golden Gate Park. Though inspired by the Japanese Tea Garden (the Hoo-den) on the Wooded Isle at the Columbian Exposition in Chicago, the San Francisco version was more elaborate in design and far more authentic. The man who envisaged and planned the Village was, ironically, an Australian named George Turner Marsh who had long studied Japanese culture and language and had opened San Francisco's first store for the sale of Asian arts at the Palace Hotel in 1876. He was also a leading real estate developer of land to the immediate north of Golden Gate Park, an area Marsh called the Richmond District (after a suburb in his native city of Melbourne). Marsh hired Japanese craftsmen to erect a magnificent gateway, a thatch and wood tea room, and a three story theatre in which a troupe of Japanese jugglers performed. In addition, he hired Japanese landscapers to surround the building with bonsai trees and plants, ponds, bridges, paths, benches and colorful lanterns. Even the thickly needled fir trees which served as a backdrop for the Tea Garden were thinned to create the illusion of Japanese firs. Admission to the Village was twenty-five cents. Patrons who wished to take refreshments were served tea by young Japanese women attired in striking ceremonial kimonos. The Japanese Tea Garden was so popular an attraction at the exposition that the Golden Gate Park Commissioners purchased it from Marsh at the fair's end and it has since remained one of San Francisco's most beloved possessions.

Mechanical Arts Building

THE MECHANICAL ARTS BUILDING which stood at the south-eastern side of the Court of Honor was the second largest building at the exposition, measuring 300 feet in length by 160 feet in width, spanning slightly over one square acre. Its architect, Edmund R. Swain, designer of McLaren Lodge in Golden Gate Park and co-designer of San Francisco's famed Ferry Building (with Arthur Page Brown), evoked the exoticism of India for the exterior of a structure whose chief purpose was to exhibit the latest advancements in industrial technology. The ivory-colored building, constructed at a cost of $75,000, sported multicolored mural decorations and ornamental sculptural reliefs along with corner turrets and two 120 feet high fluted pinnacles flanking the main entrance. The illusion of a rajah's palace was completed by ornate decorations above the building's four entrances, flags fluttering in the wind at the roofline and two elaborate kiosks at the front entrance used by fairgoers to ogle the passing crowds. The barn-like interior was comprised of a large central exhibition area at ground level with a 30 feet wide gallery 18 feet above. Included among the exhibits were steam engines and electric dynamos which powered the lights, fountains and amusement rides at the exposition. Spectators were dazzled by exhibits from General Electric, Western Electric and Southern Pacific, among other industrial giants. On view were dynamos using both Tesla's alternating current and Edison's direct current, railroad locomotives, streetcars, mammoth stamping machines, steamship assemblies, the latest in mining machinery and a fully operating bakery. The site of the Mechanical Arts Building is now occupied by the Academy of Sciences and the Steinhart Aquarium.

H. S. CROCKER COMPANY S. F.

45

Chinese Building

THOUGH MANY FOREIGN NATIONS sent goods to the Midwinter Fair from Chicago, almost none built individual pavilions to exhibit their wares. The Chinese Building pictured here might seem to be a rare exception. But in two respects this was not the case. First, the Chinese Building was not constructed by the government of China but was designed by the local firm of Martens and Cottey. It was paid for and erected at a cost of $12,000 by wealthy Chinese merchants in San Francisco as a gesture of pride in their contributions to the city's history and economic life. Second, this structure was not an exhibition hall, but an emporium where everything was for sale. Here one could buy products imported to San Francisco from China, such as plants shaped like birds and animals, joss houses made of colored paper, wooden models of junks, dolls, ebony and ivory carvings, beautifully embroidered tapestries and gowns, and silk garments of all description. The first floor and upper gallery of the building contained a bazaar, a restaurant and a tea house. At the rear of the structure was a theater where a troupe of Chinese child actors, "present, to the accompaniment of a fearfully weird orchestra, interminable and incomprehensible tragedies and comedies." The exterior was colorfully rendered in gold, red and green and the second story walls were adorned with designs of dragons and other mythical creatures. Lanterns in many shapes hung from the eaves. The steeply sloped roof dramatically extended itself beyond the walls and was punctuated by upswept scrolled horns at the corners. A pagoda-like structure rising from the middle of the roof completed the vision of an edifice emblematic of traditional Chinese style. The Chinese Building, managed by San Franciscan Leong Lam, was located directly behind the Mechanical Arts Building, significantly, among the amusements on the Midway Plaisance.

Southern California Building

THIS ILLUSTRATION CONTAINS revealing images of the cultural diversity and historical eclecticism of the Midwinter Fair and the culture which created it. In the background looms the Southern California Building whose architecture reflects both Mission Revival style in its mock bell tower beneath the flag over the righthand entrance and in the low arcades on the structure's wings (visible on the lefthand side behind the trees), as well as Mexican Hacienda influences in its red tile roof, wooden balcony and decorative reliefs around the windows and main entrance. In the middleground is the dense, English style landscape of trees, bushes and shrubs which illustrates Golden Gate Park's "Designed Wilderness" ambience. The Southern California Building stood on a rise to the north of the Court of Honor and was approached on a path lined with palms and orange trees between the Horticultural and Fine Arts Buildings. It was constructed at a cost of $20,000 to house exhibits from Los Angeles, San Diego, San Bernardino, Riverside and Ventura Counties. Because of the number of exhibitors, this structure was the largest of the many county buildings at the fair, measuring 60 feet long, 95 feet wide and covering 20,000 square feet. Upon entering the building the fairgoer passed beneath an imposing archway of oranges, underscoring the importance of the citrus industry in the Southern California of 1894. Los Angeles products dominated the interior space just as agricultural displays dominated the exhibits. Typical of mammoth food sculptures at earlier expositions, a life-size elephant made completely of walnuts, a gigantic ear of corn created from 45 bushels of normal corn ears, a Ferris Wheel of oranges turned by an electric motor, and a 23 foot pagoda of beans with 120 different varieties interwoven into the design confronted the visitor. In addition, more mundane displays such as wines, olives, fish, sugar beets, marmalades, raisins, honey and ostrich eggs could be viewed. Because of the perishables present in the pavilion, an immense amount of labor was expended in keeping the exhibits fresh and inoffensive at all times.

Grand Court of Honor Looking Southwest

THIS VIEW OF THE Grand Court of Honor taken from the roadway in front of the Manufactures and Liberal Arts Building at mid-morning (note that the shadow of the Electric Tower falls to the west) shows the full 1200 foot sweep of the area which was the main hub of the exposition. It also reveals the nine foot slope to the floor of the central part of the Court, a configuration which might have been inspired by the great central Basin at the Columbian Exposition. The sparseness of the landscaping and sculptural monuments indicates the haste with which the Midwinter Fair was created. Dominating the scene is the Electric Tower which stood slightly less than one third the height of its model, the Eiffel Tower created for the Parisian exposition of 1889. Apparent is the detailed steel fretwork of the tower to which electric bulbs were attached creating complex and changing patterns for the nightly light shows that were a popular feature of the fair. Also visible is a large searchlight atop the tower which was made in Germany and had been shown at the Columbian Exposition. It was reputed to be one of the most powerful lights in existence. Beyond the Electric Tower is Rupert Schmid's "Allegorical Fountain," a mountainous sculptural representation of symbols of California history, commerce, agriculture and mining. Directly behind the elaborate fountain looms the fanciful Administration Building. To the far left is part of the Mechanical Arts Building and a group of smallish county and Midway structures. To the far right is one of the two sphinxes which stood in front of the Fine Arts Building, the Horticultural and Agricultural Building, the Japanese Village (not visible), the Rumania, Servia (sic), Montenegro Pavilion, county buildings, and a small circular restaurant just to the right of the Administration Building. In the far distance to the right rises Strawberry Hill on top of which stood an astronomical observatory, later destroyed in the earthquake of 1906. This lithograph shows the first panoramic view visitors would have as they entered the fairgrounds through the Tenth Avenue gate on the north side of Golden Gate Park.

Oriental Village

FOR A MERE FIFTEEN CENTS wide-eyed westerners could visit the exotic quarters of the Turk, Arab, Berber, and Nubian, all people whose cultures were little known in the United States. The attraction, called the Oriental Village, had already appeared at Paris in 1889 and Chicago in 1893, but San Franciscans were smitten by the strange collection of Middle Eastern bazaar, Turkish theater and dance hall, Cairo Street, and luxuriant cafes where one might sample potent Turkish coffees and pungent Egyptian cigarettes, while reclining on a silk-cushioned ottoman. Or, as the *Official Guide* to the exposition put it, " . . . it is a succession of scenes from the 'Thousand and One Nights.' Here are the narrow roadways hemmed in by the queer architecture of the Orient, mosques with bubble-like domes, spires and minarets, gateways with carved and gilded gratings and overhanging balconies, gems of the ironworkers' art." Fairgoers found much to spend their money on in the Village. There were 60 shops selling colored silks, embroidered muslins, jeweled weapons, lamps of brass and copper, silver ornaments and, of course, Oriental carpets. In addition there were rides on camels and donkeys or in sedan chairs, theatrical performances and mock duels among Arab warriors. But most riveting for the prim Victorian visitor were the many strange and suggestive dances performed by agile young women in diaphanous attire. A stroll down Cairo Street brought into view jugglers, fire eaters, acrobats, and other performers. This side-show atmosphere, present in so many of the Asian, African, Middle Eastern and native exhibits, provided visitors to the fair with a distorted notion of non-western societies, one which separated the "serious endeavors" of Americans from the quaint exotica practised by "less civilized" cultures.

53

Manufactures and Liberal Arts Building

THE MANUFACTURES AND LIBERAL ARTS BUILDING anchored the northeastern end of the Grand Court of Honor. Like the Administration Building, it was the work of the fair's chief architect, Arthur Page Brown. However, unlike the compact and vertically oriented structure Brown designed for the exposition's administrative offices, the Manufactures and Liberal Arts Building, erected at a cost of $113,600, was a long, sprawling building measuring 462 feet in length by 225 feet in width, covering an area of about three square acres. It was not only the largest edifice at the Midwinter Fair, but also the biggest structure ever built in California. Though it was substantially smaller than earlier American exposition buildings at Philadelphia and Chicago, visitors were greatly impressed by an exhibition hall whose vertical wood and iron piers soared 92 feet, whose roof trusses spanned 158 feet, and whose walls and ceiling contained 14,000 square feet of glass. Modeled on the Roman basilica and on the Palais de l'Industrie in Paris with a tall central aisle flanked by two smaller side aisles, the Manufactures and Liberal Arts Building, like all the major exposition structures, had walls made of a special plaster material called "staff" which had been concocted to make temporary architecture look more or less permanent. For the building's exterior design Brown borrowed heavily from the vocabulary of Middle Eastern architecture, as he had also done in the Administration Building. Conforming to Midwinter Fair Director-General Michael H. de Young's admonition to avoid Classical style, he created a cream-colored façade that featured such Moorish touches as the impressive 130 feet high blue dome over the main entrance, the keyhole windows on the corner pavilions, and the Arabic design window over the main portal, (the liberal use of Gothic trefoil and quartrefoil decoration around windows and on the roofline), along with a rich palette of creams, reds, turquoises and golds. However, true to the Victorian eclecticism so apparent at the fair, Brown also included a roof of red tile, domed corner towers, and a monastery-like arcade along the southern and northern sides of the building, all examples of the California Mission style. The building's massive interior was transected by two wide avenues, giving uncluttered access to the thousands of exhibits.

Fine Arts Building

ADDING TO THE ARCHITECTURAL ECLECTICISM of the Mid-winter Fair was the exhibition hall dedicated to the fine arts. Designer C. C. McDougal, least prominent of the exposition architects, chose the Egypt of the pharaohs as his point of reference for the structure that housed the large collection of sculpture and paintings displayed at the fair. The smallest of the major exposition buildings, the Fine Arts hall cost $57,400 to construct and was originally 120 feet long by 60 feet wide. However the collection it was meant to contain quickly outgrew this space and a 40 foot wide annex had to be added to the rear of the building. Standing on a four foot rise at the northern corner of the Grand Court of Honor on a site now largely occupied by the de Young Museum, the Fine Arts Building combined elements from many of the great monuments along the Nile River, including royal temples, pyramids and sphinxes. The two story façade was created by massive corner piers supporting a corniced entablature 90 feet wide. Behind pairs of free-standing columns were the doorway and front windows. The piers, columns and entablature were covered with hieroglyphs, sculpted palms and lotuses, and reliefs of gods and mythological figures. Above the cornice sat a pyramid half the height of the façade beneath. Completing the effect of dynastic splendor were two sphinxes guarding the main approach to the building and a small forest of palm trees. The materials out of which the Fine Arts Building was made were iron and wood for trussing, plaster for walls, and glass for the ceiling. The interior, like those of the other exhibition halls, consisted of a large viewing area on the first floor and a spacious, overhanging gallery on the second. Most of the art works shown were solidly in the Romantic and Victorian traditions favored by the nineteenth century. San Francisco would have to wait until the Panama-Pacific International Exhibition of 1915 to get its first taste of modern art exhibits. In the main section of the building were displayed marble and bronze sculpture, water colors, engravings, etchings, drawings and carved gemstones. Oil paintings were exhibited in the annex at the rear. After the Midwinter Exposition closed in July of 1894, the Fine Arts Building became San Francisco's first public art museum, the de Young. It served as the museum until 1921 and was eventually demolished in 1928.

Grand Court of Honor Looking Northeast

THIS ILLUSTRATION DEMONSTRATES both the strengths and weaknesses of the Midwinter Fair. In it are depicted massive exhibition halls, grand fountains, soaring steel towers and wheels, all designed and built in a breathtaking five months. But also the meager landscaping and large unfilled spaces are all too apparent. By contrast to the Columbian Exposition a year before, the San Francisco fairgrounds reveal the effects of rapid planning and hurried construction. The Grand Court of Honor was 1200 feet long and 500 feet across. A roadway 60 feet wide circled the Court itself whose floor level was nine feet lower. In this view we see the basin of the great "Allegorical Fountain" in the right foreground, two information and souvenir kiosks in the center foreground, a statue of Christopher Columbus sent from Chicago, the 266 foot high Bonet Electrical Tower, the Manufactures and Liberal Arts Building at the upper left, the Kaiser Franz Josef Hall at the upper right, and the Mechanical Arts Building with the 100 foot high Firth Wheel peeping over its shoulder at center right. There were three observation platforms on the Electric Tower, the lowest at 80 feet, where the Belvista Cafe was located, and the highest at 210 feet. These observation areas which offered unprecedented views of the city, the Bay Area and, on clear days, even the Farallon Islands 30 miles out in the Pacific were made accessible to fairgoers by an electric elevator designed by the famed Otis Company. Today the Grand Court is the site of the Music Concourse in Golden Gate Park and is bordered by the de Young Museum, the Academy of Sciences, the Steinhart Aquarium and the Spreckels Music Stand.

Administration Building

THE ADMINISTRATION BUILDING, designed by popular San Francisco architect Arthur Page Brown whose local accomplishments included the Ferry Building and Trinity Church, housed the offices of the exposition's department chiefs. Many visitors regarded it as the Midwinter Fair's most visually stunning structure. This whimsical edifice occupied the southeastern end of the Grand Court of Honor, directly opposite Brown's monumental Manufactures and Liberal Arts Building. Constructed for $30,654, the Administration Building comprised a central square structure with domed, hexagonal pavilions at each corner, and a 135 foot high domed tower in the center. Pink, gold, cream, and white, the richly ornamented design was a riot of Arabic, Byzantine and Gothic styles. Islamic architecture inspired the great horseshoe window over the central portal, the keyhole windows at all levels of the façade and the tower pinnacles. The four bronze gilt pavilion domes and the great central dome evoked Byzantine antecedents. The complex quatrefoil decoration at the rooflines of the main building and central tower recalled Gothic style. The interior of the Administration Building stood three stories high with a majestic rotunda in the center, surrounded by galleries and loggias. Taken as a totality, Brown's edifice was a striking example of the eclecticism which dominated San Francisco's domestic architecture in the Victorian era. The site where the Administration Building once stood is now occupied by the Spreckels Music Stand.

The Mexican Band

The Eighth Regimental Band of the Mexican Army played at numerous events, including the closing ceremonies on the Fourth of July, during their six-week tenure at the fair. Along with the exposition's own official band and John Philip Sousa's Concert Band, present at the fair during the first six weeks, the Mexican ensemble provided music for special occasions as well as performing regular concerts.

Problems And Solutions

DESPITE THE PRIDE and enthusiasm which the exposition engendered, the Midwinter Fair was not without its problems. There was, of course, the ongoing resentment of W. W. Stow, John McLaren, and their supporters who felt that the exposition desecrated Golden Gate Park. But there were other difficulties that arose at the fair itself. During one of the animal shows a lion turned on his trainer and mauled him to death.[27] An Eskimo child died from hereditary syphilis in the "Esquimaux" village. To the consternation of citizens who learned of the fact later, the child was buried in Golden Gate Park by the Eskimos, without the knowledge of Park or exposition officials.[28]

The exposition suffered one major scandal during its closing days. The Society for the Suppression of Vice, ever vigilant to keep the exposition wholesome, was scandalized to learn that there was to be a nude dancer at a special event held at the exposition aquarium. The *San Francisco Examiner* reported the incident with a mixture of gusto and disapprobation:

INDECENCY ON THE MIDWAY
ONE OF THE LEWD EXHIBITIONS AT THE FAIR RAIDED.
TWO MEN WERE ARRESTED.

The indecency of the danse du ventre and the grossness of the hula-hula were eclipsed last evening by an exhibition at the close of the Midwinter Fair which it is not permitted in the columns of a daily newspaper to describe, further than by saying that the dancer was a nude woman. This disgusting performance took place before 300 men at Alexander Badlam's Aquarium on the Midway. A similar exhibition had been given on Saturday evening without interference, but the police were forced to make arrests on the night of the Sabbath, as their attention had been called to what was going on. The performances were given under the patronage of the Executive Committee appointed by the Committee of Fifty to conduct the Fair. Guards were cheering, the whistles blowing and the band playing "Auld Lang Syne," under the windows of the offices occupied by the Executive Committee. The police were attempting to hold a mad crowd that was breaking the doors and windows of the aquarium in a wild endeavor to escape arrest.

OPENLY ANNOUNCED

The spielers openly announced the event on the Midway, soliciting all who were willing to pay 50 cents, the price of admission, and in consequence the crowd was there. The majority of those on the benches were well-dressed attorneys, merchants and clerks . . .

There was no thought of danger. The woman was to dance at the Midwinter Fair after full announcement. This gave rise to the feeling of security so plainly evident . . .

When the place could hold no more a smooth-shaven person stepped to the front, smilingly mounted a chair and shouted, "All is ready." The announcement was followed by a few words of warning to the "gents," who were requested to keep quiet and remove their hats. After this he disappeared.

A DISGUSTING EXHIBITION

The sound of a violin drew attention once more to the curtain which at the same moment was pulled aside revealing a woman seated on a chair enveloped in a dark cloak. At the sound of the music she sprang to her feet revealing herself perfectly nude. She was about twenty years of age. Her head and face were veiled in a thin black scarf. She thus displayed herself for a few moments. Suddenly the sound of the violin ceased and the "dancer" sank into her chair. A moment later some one sprang upon the stage and said: "You are under arrest." There was a deathly stillness. Then the girl said in a matter-of-fact way, "All right."

A RUSH FOR THE DOOR

. . . One mad rush was made for the doors. Chairs cracked and smashed, men fell and were trampled on, blows were struck and the air resounded with curses. In the twinkling of an eye the place was cleared just as a squad of officers of the Society for the Prevention of Vice rushed in.

. . . With her were two spectators who were captured while trying to escape, but were unable to get clear with the rest. Two men were secured, but only one was charged at the police station.

Baker's Chocolate Building

It was increasingly the case in the late nineteenth century that major manufacturing houses built their own exposition pavilions rather than exhibiting in the large general halls. Baker's Chocolate had constructed its own building at Chicago and did the same at the Midwinter Fair. Here, in an ornate Levantine pavilion whose façade sported four great elephant heads (despite the western hemisphere origins of chocolate), waitresses costumed like dairymaids tended to the sweet tooth of the fairgoer. "La Belle Chocolatiére," or dairymaid, had appeared in Baker advertising since 1862. Another example of this Baker trademark appears next to one of the pavilion's windows.

The Exposition officials knew that the performance was to be given, but no steps were taken to prevent it or to have it modified.

The tickets sold at the door on Saturday night were the official tickets of the exposition, and one of the Exposition cash-girls was stationed at the door to take the tickets and see that the percentage of the receipts went to the Fair's treasury.[29]

The scandal died down in the wake of the closing ceremonies. But the one man who was charged with "attending an indecent performance"—according to one account he alone failed to escape because he was overweight and slow to flee—undoubtedly recalled the incident long after the Midwinter Fair closed its gates.

Other difficulties resonated with the international tensions alive in the decade before the turn of the century. At one point, the delegation from Japan strongly objected to the fair-planners' notion that local Japanese would pull visitors around the grounds in jinrikshas. This delegation vowed openly that they would kill any Japanese found degrading the honorable reputation of their nation by performing such menial tasks. The crisis was averted at the last minute by hiring Germans, who painted their faces and dressed up in Oriental costume.[30]

The Jinrikishas

The jinrikishas were brought over from Japan at great expense by George Marsh, a local entrepreneur. The Japanese government was outraged at the indignity of such menial service in a foreign land and announced that it would kill any Japanese worker found pulling the contrivance. As a result, Americans and Germans were hired, painted to look "Asiatic," and harnessed to the flower-covered jinrikishas.

A more urgent dilemma, from the standpoint of the Exposition Directors, presented itself in the business side of the fair. All vendors were supposed to turn over a percentage of their daily receipts to the Midwinter Exposition General Fund. It was widely believed, though, that the vendors were not reporting their earnings honestly. The Directors therefore devised a system of "rotating cash register clerks" to deal with the problem before it arose. Every day, a management-appointed clerk would take in all receipts from each exhibit. On the next day, the clerk would be shifted to another exhibit, in order to prevent familiarity and collusion arising between clerks and exhibitors.[31] The vendors growled at this enforced garrison. But the Directors were determined that the fair should show a profit; and the surest way of securing that profit, in their minds, was to be rigorous in the collection of its contractual receipts.

The policy paid off. When the California Midwinter International Exposition officially closed its doors on July 4, 1894, Director-General de Young could boast that the fair had accomplished all of its goals. The exposition had earned $1,260,112.19 in revenues, as against $1,193,260.70 in expenditures, netting a profit of $66,851.49, without asking for or receiving a single penny of support from federal, state, or local government sources.[32] And after the fair closed, the Fine Arts Building would remain in Golden Gate Park as the city's first municipal museum.

Best of all was the recovery of San Francisco's businesses. In the months before the fair was opened, said exposition Director-General de Young, "stagnation and business depression were everywhere. There was a threatened run on our banks, and a want of confidence was universally apparent. Look today at the situation. There is a complete restoration of confidence; business is progressing as of yore, our streets are crowded, and the general community is in a better frame of mind."[33] De Young's optimism seems to be confirmed by the fact that there were no major labor strikes in San Francisco for the remainder of the century, and by the emergence of a building boom in the years immediately after the fair, resulting in such structures as the Emporium Department Store, the new Cliff House, the Sutro Baths, and the Ferry Building.

The Tea Garden

The Japanese Tea Garden was the gem of the Japanese exhibition at the Midwinter Fair. Though much altered from its original state, the Tea Garden remains the most significant physical contribution of the exposition to the city of San Francisco.

Revenge And Restoration

BUT THERE WAS one man in San Francisco who was not in a better frame of mind. John McLaren, Superintendent of Golden Gate Park, had strenuously objected to the entire scheme of staging a world's fair in the midst of his fragile new park, begun on April 4, 1870. He watched with dismay as newly planted areas were torn up for power and water lines. Buildings were constructed in an area originally intended as a woodland retreat from urban life, and hordes of fairgoers tramped and trampled over grounds not yet able to withstand such intense usage. The businessmen had their way, and McLaren bided his time in angry silence.

After the Midwinter Fair officially closed in July, the Superintendent of Golden Gate Park had his revenge. The exposition's Board of Directors had promised to clear away all the temporary buildings within 90 days after the event was concluded. But the structures remained, as the former Directors returned to their daily concerns. By January, 1896, McLaren's patience ran out. He dynamited almost all of the remaining structures of the fair and took great delight in watching the gaudy architectural fantasies blow apart in showers of multicolored debris. The last to go was the electrical tower, shuddering and collapsing into a heap of twisted iron.

The structures he had despised for so long had been brought down. Should he remove every reminder of the hateful show? Not quite. McLaren knew a good work of landscape architecture when he saw one. The pseudo-Levantine castles could go up in smoke, the minarets and onion domes, fluted arches, and knobby finials could descend forever into the scrap heap. But the Japanese Tea Garden—the one exposition exhibit that blended best with the natural beauty of Golden Gate Park—this garden he spared. It stands today as one of the last reminders that a century ago the world came to San Francisco to see Michael de Young's remarkable vision come true. Fortunately for McLaren and his successors, the Midwinter Fair was the only international exposition ever to be held in Golden Gate Park.

The Cider Press

The *Cider Press*, one of the largest bronze statues at the fair, was yet another of the myriad symbols of California's agricultural fecundity. A classical figure strains at the screw of his press to squeeze juice from the rich fruit within. This statue stood at the northern corner of the roadway between the Fine Arts and the Manufactures and Liberal Arts Buildings (seen in the background). After the exposition ended, the *Cider Press* remained in Golden Gate Park where it can still be seen today.

The Legacy

S AN FRANCISCANS HAD every reason to be proud of the success of the California Midwinter International Exposition. Many another older, more established city in Europe and America had witnessed its illustrious exhibition end in financial ruin for backers and humiliation for the host city. Though certainly not of the magnitude of the great expositions of Chicago or Paris, the Midwinter Fair proved what it set out to prove: that San Francisco was a truly cosmopolitan city capable of planning and executing a major event with great skill.

It is not difficult to trace the effects of the exposition on the immediate environment of Golden Gate Park. For better or for worse, the exposition set the precedent of large-scale construction and traffic within the Park itself. The Midwinter Exposition provided not only the precedent, but the first building for this new complex—McDougal's Fine Arts Building, which survived until 1928. This structure became San Francisco's first de Young Museum. Part of the profit from the fair was used to buy its first major work of art—Gustave Doré's huge "Poem of the Vine" sculpture, which stood at the entrance of the de Young Museum for many years.

The story of how de Young acquired the Doré vase is a textbook example of American hardball bargain-driving in that era. The French foundrymen who had cast the vase were unable to sell it (Gustave Doré, the artist, had died in 1883, leaving the casting bill unpaid) or to recoup their expenses. They had shipped the vase first to Chicago for the Columbian Exposition, then to San Francisco for the Midwinter Fair. De Young wanted the vase very much—it seemed to him a magnificent example of French art and, with its theme of wine and wine-making, a most appropriate work for California.

The Thiebaut brothers, owners of the bronze-casting firm, needed 60,000 francs to pay for the costs of casting, storage, and transportation of the eleven-foot tall vase. They were asking 80,000 francs, but were apparently willing to settle for the 60,000 francs just to be rid of the burden.

De Young called them into his office at the *San Francisco Chronicle* and offered them 50,000 francs. They refused. After a long series of proposals and counterproposals, de Young reached into his pocket, extracted 50,000 francs, and calmly spread them out on the table in front of the Thiebaut brothers.

"Take it or leave it, gentlemen," was his final offer.

Seeing five-sixths of their longstanding debt so tangibly close for the taking proved too strong a temptation for the Frenchmen. They took the money, and Gustave Doré's vase had found a home in San Francisco.[34]

De Young's bravado bargaining and the foundation of the de Young Museum portended a great change for San Francisco's major public park. The original plan for Golden Gate Park—to serve as a wilderness within the city, a place of greenery broken only by rustic, utilitarian structures (such as stone bridges) or plant related buildings (such as the Conservatory of Flowers)—underwent a drastic revision in the wake of the Midwinter Fair. Today, where the buildings of the exposition once stood, a large academy of science, an art museum, and extensive parking lots occupy the space that the original designers of the Park planned to be a natural area reserved for music in the middle of trees and shrubs. Both the educational aspirations and the financial necessities of operating the Academy of Science and the de Young Museum necessitate coaxing large crowds of people to attend the exhibits and events there— crowds that may use Golden Gate Park only as a place to drive through on the way to some special event or school outing.

Once the buildings of an international fair are razed the story of its accomplishments remain to be rediscovered in the pages of newspapers and magazines, and in photographs. Isaiah West Taber (1830-1912) was the official photographer for the Midwinter Fair. Born in Massachusetts, he worked as a whaler, gold miner, rancher and dentist before settling into a career as a photographer in New York City. In 1864 Taber moved to California where he first worked at Bradley & Rulofson's gallery. He opened his own studio in 1871 and by 1894 was the leading portrait photographer in San Francisco. Taber and his assistants were said to have made over 5,000 negatives of exposition views.

There are other legacies as well. The Music Concourse today occupies the area excavated for the fair's Court of Honor. Several statues from the exposition—Thomas Shields Clarke's *Cider Press* (also called the *Wine Press*) and the two sphinxes among them—have survived from the fair and adorn the Music Concourse today. But the most "splendid survivor" of the Midwinter Exposition is the Japanese Tea Garden. The landscaping and the structures of the Tea Garden have changed radically in the years since its first opening; but it remains the one exhibit from the fair that most gracefully accommodates itself to the original plan of Golden Gate Park.

One of the most unusual indirect legacies of the Japanese Tea Garden was the invention of the so-called Chinese fortune cookie. Japanese landscaper Makoto Hagiwara, was hired to serve as caretaker of the Tea Garden at the close of the fair. After a falling out with Park officials, he opened another Japanese pavilion across from Golden Gate Park. In an effort to attract customers, he introduced a novel item: small, hard cookies containing slips of paper with words of wisdom or prophesy printed on them. These "fortune cookies" became instant favorites with his customers. When Hagiwara and the Park officials came to an agreement and he returned to work at the Japanese Tea Garden, he brought his innovation with him. There is, of course, some irony in the fact that the "Chinese fortune cookie" was created by a Japanese public servant in San Francisco.

The effects of the Midwinter Fair on San Francisco as a whole are more difficult to assess. The city continued to develop rapidly throughout the remaining years of the nineteenth century. But it is hard to say how much of the city's growth and prosperity can be linked directly to the influence of the fair. One of the major goals of the exposition was to showcase California's benign winter climate so that visitors might be induced to move to San Francisco and its environs. And indeed, the population of the city grew from some 300,000 to over 400,000 by the turn of the century. But it is impossible to say how many people were influenced, directly or indirectly, to make the move as a result of their experiences at, or hearsay about, the Midwinter Fair.

It seems clear that the exposition had an effect on the cultural spirit of San Francisco. The City Beautiful Movement undoubtedly drew much of its inspiration and confidence from the coordinated architecture and social idealism of international expositions. The appearance of sculptures on Market Street and throughout Golden Gate Park came as a result of the new civic taste for public monuments such as those that adorned the grounds of the Midwinter Fair.

The intellectual exchanges begun at the Fair also continued beyond the closing of the exposition itself. To cite only one example, the Afro-American Congress, held in San Francisco in July, 1895, would not have occurred without the impetus provided by the Midwinter Exposition and the activities of its Afro-American Day.

It is certain that by 1915 most people had all but forgotten about the Midwinter Fair. Planners for the great Panama-Pacific International Exposition (held in the Marina District of San Francisco) made scant reference to the previous fair. Organizers of the third world's fair, the Golden Gate International Exposition (held on the newly-created Treasure Island in 1939–1940), made even less reference to the Midwinter Fair. And certainly both the Panama Pacific International Exhibition and the Golden Gate International Exhibition outshone the Midwinter Fair in size, ambition, number of exhibitors, revenues —in short, in every category that counted. Today, most people are unaware that San Francisco's first world's fair ever occurred, so far has it faded from public memory.

But the California Midwinter International Exposition did take place. An energetic and fervent band of believers in the virtues of their city and in their own abilities managed to conjure up an entire "world's fair," complete with all the trappings, in an astonishingly short time. The kind of élan that comes with such a success cannot be easily measured; but it is no less real for that. San Francisco's reputation as the "city that knows how," a place where serious enterprise and fun can go hand in hand, was richly deserved in 1894. The effects of such a success surely outlived the closing ceremonies of the exposition. And, in the longer view of San Francisco's history, the phenomenal spirit and energy which produced an international exposition in slightly more than seven months, are revealing harbingers of the remarkable way in which the city would reconstruct itself in the wake of the cataclysm that befell it a mere twelve years later in 1906.

ENDNOTES

1. See Marvin Nathan, "San Francisco's Fin de Siécle Bohemian Renaissance," *California History*, Volume LXI, No. 3 (Fall, 1982), 196-209.

2. *San Francisco Chronicle*, June 1, 1893, page 1.

3. These cards could well presage the New York *vs.* California debates that continue to rage today.

4. *Official History of the California Midwinter International Exposition*, (H. S. Crocker Company: San Francisco, 1895), page 37.

5. *San Francisco Call*, July 14, 1893, page 4.

6. See Raymond Clary, *The Making of Golden Gate Park: The Early Years: 1865-1906* (California Living Books: San Francisco, 1980), page 112. The newsboys were properly acknowledged for their modest contribution. On March 30, 1894, they had their own parade, which began in the downtown area and concluded at the fairgrounds. See the *Riverside Daily Press*, March 30, 1894, page 3.

7. Sometimes unlikely historical accidents become a mainstay of tradition. The outer buttressing of the Parisian Palace of Industry was a result of a failure of nerve on the part of the designers. Afraid that the slender iron supports would not sustain the heavy sheets of glass, they buttressed the exterior with stone casings. The San Francisco Manufactures and Liberal Arts Building was sheathed only with staff, a kind of plaster-of-Paris useful for temporary covering. Staff has little or no structural integrity. And by 1894, the structural capabilities of iron were well-known, and stone buttressing was unnecessary. But because that Parisian Palace of Industry had had a monumental wall, San Francisco's Palace would have its wall, too.

8. *Official History*, page 51.

9. We have been unable to find records of any public debate over the destruction of the Fine Arts Palace in 1928. The newspapers are silent. The Park Commissioners did not even take out a demolition permit from the city—a usual requirement in such matters. They must have felt the act was so self-evidently necessary and agreed-upon that city officials need not be notified. It is likely that by 1928 the Egyptian Revival style was not only out of favor, it was openly ridiculed, and stood as an embarrassing reminder of the quirky taste of city officials at the end of the nineteenth century. In addition, the structure leaked constantly, and some of the works therein (notably the stuffed animals) had suffered damage. Mulgardt's new de Young Museum, far larger and more in accordance with the taste of the 1920s, rendered the old building superfluous.

10. Bonet, the designer of the Tower, may have secretly incorporated his opinion of the Midwinter Fair into his structure. The Bonet Tower was 266 feet high. The Eiffel Tower, constructed in 1889 for the Exposition Universelle in Paris, rose 300 meters into the sky. "Thus are these American ventures to our French," Bonet may be saying. "As three hundred feet is to three hundred meters, so is America to France!"

11. *Official History*, page 155.

12. *Official History*, page 131.

13. *Official Catalogue: A Reference Book of Exhibitors and Exhibits* (San Francisco, 1894), page 20.

14. See Arthur Chandler, "The Towers of San Francisco," *World's Fair*, Summer, 1984, 5-6.

15. *The Wasp—Midwinter Edition*, Volume XXXII, No. 4 (January 27, 1894), page 10. After the close of the exposition, Dante's Inferno was purchased at a bargain rate by a local bar-owner. The *San Francisco Chronicle* reported on October 22, 1894:

> Dante's Inferno was bought by Haggarty—the same Haggarty whose Shebeon just outside the gate at the State University grounds had made his name a common thing in the petty criminal records of Berkeley. His bill of sale read: 'Hell and its present contents $12.50.' Temperance people will say that the purchase was appropriate. The dragon at the entrance has lost its fury. His teeth are dropping out. The iconoclastic carpenters are tearing away his bat-like wings.

16. *Ibid.*

17. "Hawaii Village: A Fair in Itself," *The Wasp*, op. cit., page 10.

18. "Old Maid's Diary," *The Illustrated Wasp*, May 26, 1894, page 12.

19. *Mendocino Beacon*, February 3, 1894, page 3.

20. *Los Angeles Times*, January 21, 1894, page 3.

21. Odd as these organic sculptures might seem to us today, they were a distinct improvement on the Venus de Milo sculpted from a one ton chunk of chocolate that the Americans exhibited in Paris at the 1889 exposition universelle. As the warm days progressed, the confectionery goddess warped and crumpled into a grotesque parody of Greek art. All one French critic could say of the chocolate Venus was that "she is inexpressibly American."

22. *Sacramento Daily Record-Union*, September 20, 1893, page 2.

23. *San Francisco Daily Report*, June 5, 1894.

24. *San Francisco Chronicle*, June 6, 1894, page 5.

25. *Ibid.*, page 5. The first "Negro Building" would be erected the next year, 1895, at the Cotton States and International Exhibition, held in Atlanta, Georgia.

26. *Ibid.*

27. *Official History*, page 159.

28. *Ibid.*, page 256.

29. *San Francisco Examiner*, July 1894.

30. See illustrations in the *Official History*, pages 25 and 165.

31. "Report on the Department of Concessions," *Official History*, page 235.

32. *Official History*, page 214.

33. *Ibid.*, page 76

34. Accounts vary as to the actual amount offered by de Young, but all agree that he drove a hard bargain with the Frenchmen.

STATISTICAL APPENDIX

OFFICIAL NAME: The California Midwinter International Exposition

DATES: Open January 27, 1894; closed July 4, 1894

LOCATION: Golden Gate Park, San Francisco

SIZE OF EXHIBITION GROUNDS: 160 acres

DIRECTOR: Michael H. de Young

RECEIPTS: $1,260,112.19

DISBURSEMENTS: $1,193,260.70

TOTAL PAID ATTENDANCE: 1,315,002 persons

FREE ADMISSIONS: 904,148 persons

EXHIBITING FOREIGN COUNTRIES: 18

EXHIBITING STATES: 5

BIBLIOGRAPHY

The major collections of Midwinter Exposition material are the Museum of the City of San Francisco which houses the Raymond Clary Collection, the richest single source of written and ephemeral material relating to the Fair; the Special Collections Room of the San Francisco Public Library which holds numerous documents, including a copy of the Taber volume of exposition photographs; and the Special Collections Room of the Henry Madden Library at California State University in Fresno. This latter collection is the best single source for materials on all international expositions from 1851 to 1939.

— *All About the Midwinter Fair*. San Francisco: W. B. Bancroft & Co., 1894.

—*Ansichten von Californien und der California Midwinter International Exposition*. [No place or date of publication.]

Athearn, S. and Stone, K. E. *Midwinter Fair Cookbook*. San Francisco: Press of Mysell and Rollins. [No date of publication.]

Bamford, Mary E. *The Denby Children at the Fair*. Elgin, Ill.: Cook Publishing Co., 1904. [A story set at the Midwinter Fair.]

Barth, Gunther. "California Midwinter International Exposition," in *West Coast Expositions and Galas*, Samuel Stark, ed. San Francisco: The Book Club of California, 1970.

Bates, Elizabeth S. "Some Breadwinners of the Fair," *Overland Monthly*, XXIII: 33 (April 1894), 374-384.

—*Berkeley Weekly Herald*. [Articles on Berkeley's participation in the Midwinter Exposition were published on October 5, November 30 and December 21, 1893 and January 18, 1894.]

Birt, Rodger. "Pictures of an Exposition: Isaiah W. Taber and the San Francisco Midwinter Fair," *Humanities Journal* (1986), 7-10.

—*The Books of the Fairs. Materials about World's Fairs, 1834-1916, in the Smithsonian Institution Libraries*. Introductory Essay by Robert W. Rydell. Chicago & London: American Library Association, 1992, 175-176.

Brill, Dick. "Fair was cure for economic doldrums," *The Progress* (July 2, 1976), 7-9. [Retrospective on Midwinter Fair.]

—*California International Exposition Musical Keepsake*. Boston: John C. Haynes & Co., 1894.

—*California Midwinter Exposition Illustrated Series of the Pacific States: The Authentic Pictorial Journal of the Exposition*. [A newspaper published for the exposition by the Illustrated Publishing Company between March and July of 1894. It was issued as a bimonthly in March and April and as a monthly from May to July.]

—*California Midwinter Exposition Hotel Directory*. Vol. 1, No. 2, February 3, 1894. San Francisco: F. S. Wilson.

—*California Midwinter Exposition Illustrated* (official souvenir). San Francisco: H. S. Crocker Co., 1894.

—*California Midwinter International Exposition*, San Francisco, January 1st to June 30th, 1894. Portland, Me.: Leighton & Frey Souvenir View Co., 1894.

—*California Midwinter International Exposition, "Nutshell Guide."* [No publication information. Contains illustrations and descriptions of fair sites.]

Chandler, Arthur. "A Victorian Melodrama: The Poem of the Vine," *World's Fair* III, 1 (Spring, 1983), 12-14.

Chandler, Arthur. "San Francisco's Fantastic Fair of 1894," *World's Fair* VI, 1 (Winter, 1986), 13-16.

Chandler, Arthur. "The Towers of San Francisco," *World's Fair* V, 3 (Summer, 1985), 5-6.

Clary, Raymond H. *The Making of Golden Gate Park: The Early Years: 1865-1906.* San Francisco: California Living Books, 1980. "Midwinter Fair," 356-370.

—*Das Goethe-Schiller Denkmal in San Francisco, California. Erinnerungen an den "Deutschen Tag" der California Midwinter International Exposition, 1894 und das "Goethe-Schiller Fest" 1895 und an die "Enthullung des Denkmals" im Golden Gate park, 1901.* San Francisco: 1901.

De Young, Michael H. "Benefits of the Midwinter Exposition," *The Californian* (March, 1894).

—Dickman-Jones Co. *California Midwinter International Exposition, 1894.* San Francisco: San Francisco Morning Call, 1894.

—M. H. de Young Memorial Museum. "Story of Midwinter Exposition," San Francisco: Golden Gate Park Commission Publication, 1921. 10-18.

Eames, Ninetta. "The Wild and Woolly at the Fair," *Overland Monthly,* XXIII: 33 (April 1894), 356-370.

Evans, Taliesin. *All About the Midwinter Fair, San Francisco, and Interesting Facts Concerning California.* 2nd ed. San Francisco: W. B. Bancroft & Co., 1894.

—*Exposition Catalogue of Santa Clara College.* Santa Clara: 1894.

Findling, John E., and Pelle, Kimberly D., eds. *Historical Dictionary of World's Fairs and Expositions,* 1851-1988. New York: Greenwood Press, 1990, 135-136.

—*Golden Gate Park News and Official Program (Midwinter Exposition Edition),* August 24, 1893.

Graham, C. *Official Portfolio of the California Midwinter International Exposition.* San Francisco: Winter's Art Litho Company. [No date but surely 1894.]

Graham, C. *Water Color Sketches of the White City and Sunset City. Color Views.* San Francisco: *San Francisco Examiner.* [No date but surely 1894.]

Hall, C. F. "The Midwinter Steal," clipping dated May 25, 1894 in the Bancroft Library, University of California, Berkeley.

Herny, Ed. *California Midwinter Fair 1894: A Magic Lantern Slide Lecture by Ed Herny. Privately published by Ed Herny,* 1986. [Contains a list of 70 magic lantern slides of the fair.]

—"Illustrations," *California Architect and Building News,* Vol XIV, No. 9 (September, 1893), 102ff. [Sketches of Second Prize winners for design of main exhibition halls.]

—*In Remembrance of the Midwinter International Exposition: San Francisco, 1894. A book of illustrative lithographs.* San Francisco: Hergert & Frey, 1894.

—*Information for Intending Exhibitors* [at the Midwinter Fair.] San Francisco: 1893.

—*Los Angeles Times,* January-June, 1894. various issues.

Loy, Daniel Oscar. *Poems of the Golden State and Midwinter Exposition.* San Francisco, 1894.

—*Mendocino Beacon,* February 3, 1894.

—*Midwinter Appeal and Journal of '94.* [A newspaper regularly published at the fairgrounds.]

—*Midwinter Fair and the Golden State. Art Views.* San Francisco: H. S. Crocker Co., 1894. [Includes color views.]

—*Midwinter Fair Daily.* [A newspaper published each day at the fair.]

—*Midwinter Scenes in Golden Gate Park.* San Francisco: A. J. McDonald and Sons, 1893.

—*Monarch Souvenir of Sunset City and Sunset Scenes: Being Views of California's Midwinter Festival and Famous Scenes in the Golden State.* San Francisco, 1894.

—*Official Catalogue: A Reference Book of Exhibitors and Exhibits, Officers and Members.* 1st ed. San Francisco: Harvey, Whitcher & Allen, 1894.

—*Official Catalogue, Department of Fine Arts. John A. Stanton, Chief.* San Francisco: Harvey, Whitcher & Allen, 1894.

—*Official Guide to the California Midwinter Exposition.* San Francisco: George Spaulding and Company, 1894.

—*Official History of the California Midwinter Exposition.* San Francisco: Press of H. S. Crocker Company, 1894.

—*Official Souvenir of the California Midwinter International Exposition.* San Francisco: R. A. Irving, 1894.

Phelan, James D. "Is the Midwinter Fair a Benefit?" *Overland Monthly* XXIII: 33 (April, 1894), 390-392.

—*Reno Evening Gazette*, February 19, 1894.

—*Riverside Daily Press*, March 30, 1894.

—*Sacramento Daily Record-Union.* September, 1893-June, 1894; various issues.

—*San Francisco Chronicle, Examiner* and *Morning Call*, from December 1893 to July, 1894. [All newspapers printed special fair editions plus many stories. Among the *Chronicle* articles are: "Scenes at the Fair" (Jan. 1, 1894); "The Fair's First Day" (Jan. 2, 1894); "Turned Out on Time" (Jan. 5, 1894); "Preparing to Open" (Jan. 7, 1894); "The Day has been Set" (Jan. 11, 1894); "Inaugural Congress" (Jan. 26, 1894); "Immense Crowd" (July 5, 1894). The exposition congresses were fairly thoroughly summarized in a series of articles running in the *Chronicle* from April 15 to June 13, 1894.]

—*Scientific American* (April 14, 21, June 16, 23, and July 14, 1894). [These articles deal with the architecture, the landscaping and the scientific and technological exhibits at the fair.]

—*Sunset City and Sunset Scenes, No. 2, May 14, 1894.* San Francisco: T. C. Russel Co., 1894.

—-United Brotherhood of Labor. "Facts Concerning the Midwinter Fair." San Francisco: Sept. 9, 1894.

—*U. S. Mail Official Postal Guide. Midwinter Fair Souvenir of the Letter Carriers of San Francisco 1893-1894.* Washington, D. C.: Post Office Department, 1894.

—*The Wasp.* "Midwinter Edition," Vol. XXXII, No. 4 (January 27, 1894). [Other articles appeared in *The Wasp* on March 10 and May 26, 1894.]

Weaver, Phil, Jr. "Going With the Swim," *Overland Monthly* XXIII: 33 (April 1894), 414-420.

—*Welcome to Our California Midwinter International Exposition. Compliments of the City of Paris.* San Francisco: no date.

—*Welcome to our California Midwinter International Exposition. Souvenir.* Oakland: Abrahamson Co., Inc., 1894.

—*West Coast Expositions and Galas. Number Four in the Series of Keepsakes.* San Francisco: The Book Club of California, 1970. [Includes a series of brief articles on Western expositions and celebrations from 1894 to 1915.]

Witteman, Adolph. *The California Midwinter International Exposition in Photogravure.* New York: A. Wittemann; San Francisco: Joseph A. Hoffman. [No date but surely 1894.]

Index